MADAM&E

MADAMS are from MARS

MAIDS ARE FROM VENUS

by S.Francis, H. Dugmore & Rico

PENGUIN BOOKS

PENGUIN BOOKS

Published by the Penguin Group
80 Strand, London WC2R 0RL, England
Penguin Putnam Inc, 375 Hudson Street, New York, New York 10014, USA
Penguin Books Australia Ltd, 250 Camberwell Road, Camberwell, Victoria 3124, Australia
Penguin Books Canada Ltd, 10 Alcorn Avenue, Toronto, Ontario, Canada M4V 3B2
Penguin Books (NZ) Ltd, Cnr Rosedale and Airborne Roads, Albany, Auckland, New Zealand
Penguin Books India (P) Ltd, 11 Community Centre, Panchsheel Park, New Delhi – 110 017, India
Penguin Books (South Africa) (Pty) Ltd, 24 Sturdee Avenue, Rosebank, Johannesburg 2196, South Africa

Penguin Books (South Africa) (Pty) Ltd, Registered Offices:
Second Floor, 90 Rivonia Road, Sandton 2196, South Africa

First published by Penguin Books (South Africa) (Pty) Ltd 1997
Reprinted 1998
This edition published by Penguin Books 2002

ISBN 0 143 02425 6

Reproduction by Interpak Books
Printed and bound by Interpak Books, Pietermaritzburg

MADAM&EVE

"HIDE THE VACUUM CLEANER AND GET OUT THE OVEN MITTS!"
"Vibrant satire with praise and acclaim from all corners of South Africa."
-The Saturday Star

"THE COUNTRY'S BEST KNOWN CARTOON STRIP."
"... Plays on the absurdities of South African race relations."
-The Economist

"SOUTH AFRICA'S FAVOURITE TRILOGY OF TERROR."
"Madam & Eve, and the gin-swigging Mother Anderson keep going from strength to strength."
-Options Magazine

"BRILLIANT."
"... South Africa's number one cartoon strip has captured the hearts and funny bones of ordinary South Africans."
-The Sunday Times

"FIVE CHEERS FOR MADAM &EVE."
"South Africa's most successful cartoon strip has won the hearts of millions."
-The Mail & Guardian

"THEY DON'T COME MUCH BETTER THAN THIS."
"Consistently and hilariously funny."
-The Daily Dispatch

"A WHOLE LOT OF FUN!"
"... Madam & Eve has helped all South Africans laugh at themselves."
-The Eastern Province Herald

"A REFLECTION AND PART OF THE CULTURE."
"Madam & Eve are us."
-The Cape Argus

"MADAM & EVE..."
"A nation that laughs together."
-The Sunday Tribune

Other Madam & Eve books

The Madam & Eve Collection (1993)
Free at Last (Penguin Books, 1994)
All Aboard for the Gravy Train (Penguin Books, 1995)
Somewhere over the Rainbow Nation (Penguin Books, 1996)
Madam & Eve's Greatest Hits (Penguin Books, 1997)
Jamen sort kaffe er pa nu, Madam! (Gyldendal, Denmark, 1995)
Jeg giver Mandela Skylden for det her! (Gyldendal, Denmark, 1996)

Madam & Eve appears regularly in:

The Mail & Guardian, The Star, The Saturday Star, City Press,
The Eastern Province Herald, The Natal Mercury, The Natal Witness,
The Daily Dispatch, The Cape Times, The Diamond Fields Advertiser,
Die Volksblad, The Pretoria News, Zimbabwe Standard,
The S.A. Times, Fair Lady, Vodaworld, Student Life,
Ernie (Bladkompaniet A.S., Oslo) and Larson! (Atlantic Forlags AB, Stockholm)

To contact Madam & Eve:

POST: PO Box 94, WITS Post Office, 2050 South Africa
E-MAIL: madamandeve@pop.onwe.co.za
WORLD WIBE WEB: Visit Madam & Eve at the
Electronic Mail & Guardian's Web page: http://www.mg.co.za/mg/

EVE -- I BOUGHT A NEW SELF-HELP BOOK THAT I THINK COULD REALLY IMPROVE OUR RELATIONSHIP.
"MADAMS ARE FROM MARS, MAIDS ARE FROM VENUS."
I'M FROM SOWETO. MAYBE YOU CAN STILL GET A REFUND.
COULD YOU AT LEAST READ THE FIRST CHAPTER?!

THIS IS THE BOOK YOU BOUGHT? "MADAMS ARE FROM MARS, MAIDS ARE FROM VENUS."
IT'LL NEVER WORK. EVE'S FROM SOWETO.
DOES EVERYBODY HAVE TO TAKE THINGS SO LITERALLY AROUND HERE! IT'S A METAPHOR!
A METAPHOR? WELL, EXCUSE ME! I MUST BE THICK AS A BRICK.
NO! NO! THAT'S A SIMILE!

HEY! A NEW BOOK!
"MADAMS ARE FROM MARS, MAIDS ARE FROM VENUS".
NO, IT'S NOT SCIENCE FICTION.
OBVIOUSLY. THE TITLE IS A METAPHORICAL EXPRESSION CONVEYING THE VAST CULTURAL CHASM BETWEEN DOMESTIC EMPLOYERS AND EMPLOYEES.
BY THE WAY. HAVE YOU SEEN MY COLOURING-IN BOOK?

"MADAMS ARE FROM MARS, MAIDS ARE FROM VENUS... CHAPTER ONE: WHEN DEALING WITH YOUR DOMESTIC WORKER, ALWAYS BE CHEERFUL AND HAVE A POSITIVE ATTITUDE."
BAD NEWS, MADAM -- THE VACUUM CLEANER'S BROKEN.
HEY -- NO PROBLEM! YOU CAN USE THE BRUSH AND DUSTPAN!
©RAPID PHASE·1997 http://www.mg.co.za/mg/
BEAUTIFUL DAY, ISN'T IT?

"MADAMS ARE FROM MARS, MAIDS ARE FROM VENUS... CHAPTER TWO: BE SURE TO MAKE ALL WAGE NEGOTIATIONS FUN."
©RAPID PHASE·1997 http://www.mg.co.za/mg/
HI EVE. GUESS WHAT? I'LL RACE YOU TO THE KITCHEN, THE WINNER GETS A RAISE. GO.
ZIP!
ISN'T THIS FUN?!!
I WONDER IF AUTHORS STILL GET DEATH SENTENCES?

MADAM & Eve
BY S.FRANCIS, H.DUGMORE & RICO
MIELLLIES!!
SCREECH
CLICK
DALE A TU CUERPO ALEGRIA MACARENA
QUE TU CUERPO ES PA' DARLE ALEGRIA Y COSA BUENA...
DALE A TU CUERPO ALEGRIA MACARENA!
HEYYY MACARENA!!
CLICK

"MADAMS ARE FROM MARS, MAIDS ARE FROM VENUS... CHAPTER 3: NO MATTER HOW DIFFICULT, ALWAYS TRY AND **COMPLIMENT** YOUR DOMESTIC WORKER."
©RAPID PHASE-1997
http://www.mg.co.za/mg/
THIS SOUP IS DELICIOUS, EVE.
THAT'S HANDY ANDY.

"MADAMS ARE FROM MARS, MAIDS ARE FROM VENUS... CHAPTER 12: ALWAYS START THE DAY WITH A FRIENDLY SMILE."
http://www.mg.co.za/mg/
©RAPID PHASE-1997
SHE'S POISONED MY TEA.

"MADAMS ARE FROM MARS MAIDS ARE FROM VENUS... CHAPTER 14: IF YOU MUST SAY 'NO', BE COURTEOUS."
EVE ... DID YOU WASH THE DISHES?
NO. BUT THANK YOU VERY MUCH FOR ASKING.
CAN YOU TELL ME WHY YOU DIDN'T WASH THE DISHES?
NO. BUT THANK YOU VERY MUCH FOR ASKING.
http://www.mg.co.za/mg/
©RAPID PHASE-1997
HAS EVERYONE IN THIS HOUSE GONE CRAZY?!
NO. BUT THANK YOU VERY MUCH FOR ASKING.

"MADAMS ARE FROM MARS MAIDS ARE FROM VENUS... CHAPTER 16: GET TO KNOW YOUR MADAM AS A PERSON."
HI MADAM. LET'S TALK ABOUT **YOU**.
WHAT ARE YOUR **DREAMS**? YOUR **HOPES**? YOUR INNERMOST **DESIRES**? WHAT IS GWEN ANDERSON REALLY LIKE? WHAT DOES SHE WANT MORE THAN ANYTHING ELSE?
©RAPID PHASE-1997 http://www.mg.co.za/mg/
IF YOU ASK **ME**, THIS IS NO WAY TO START A BONDING EXPERIENCE!

COULD YOU MAKE IT OUT... "TO BOB?"
WITH PLEASURE.
©RAPID PHASE-1997 http://www.mg.co.za/mg/
EXCUSE ME. ARE YOU THE AUTHOR OF "MADAMS ARE FROM MARS, MAIDS ARE FROM VENUS"?
WHY YES. YES I AM.
...WHERE'S YOUR BOOK? I'LL BE HAPPY TO SIGN IT.

MOM! GUESS WHO JUST FLEW IN TO SOUTH AFRICA.
I GIVE UP.
I'LL GIVE YOU A HINT. HE'S PALE, HE DRESSES IN BLACK, HE SLEEPS IN A BOX AND CAN'T STAND SUNLIGHT.
DRACULA?
MICHAEL JACKSON!

AND NOW, WE CONTINUE WITH OUR LIVE COVERAGE OF MICHAEL JACKSON'S PILGRIMAGE TO SOUTH AFRICA.
MICHAEL HAS JUST EMERGED FROM THE AEROPLANE--HE'S KNEELING DOWN TO KISS THE SOUTH AFRICAN SOIL!
I CAN'T DO IT. THERE COULD BE GERMS.
AND NOW, ONE OF HIS HANDLERS IS KISSING IT FOR HIM.
I'M HOME!!

LOOK!! THERE HE IS! IT'S MICHAEL JACKSON!!
HURRY!
I SAW HIM FIRST!
OUT OF MY WAY!
...MEMBERS OF THE PRESS?
REAL ESTATE AGENTS.

AND IN OTHER NEWS, MICHAEL JACKSON SPENT THE DAY HOUSE-HUNTING IN SOUTH AFRICA.
STOP THE LIMO!! I FOUND IT! I FOUND MY NEW HOME!!
MICHAEL... THAT'S THE UNION BUILDING.
IT'S PERFECT! I CAN PUT THE ZOO IN THE GARDEN!

MR. PRESIDENT.. MICHAEL JACKSON WANTS TO BUY THE UNION BUILDINGS AS HIS NEW HOME.
WHAT?!
HE'S OFFERED 50 MILLION AND UNLIMITED FOREIGN INVESTMENT.
WHEN DO WE HAVE TO BE OUT?
END OF THE MONTH. BEFORE THE GIRAFFES ARRIVE.

MICHAEL JACKSON VISITS THE KRUGER NATIONAL PARK.
OVER THERE! IT'S MICHAEL JACKSON'S LIMO!
YOU'RE CRAZY. THAT'S JUST AN ANTHILL.
NO--HE'S RIGHT! SEE THAT BIG TREE? LOOK BEYOND IT!
OH YEAH! I SEE IT! I SEE IT!

MADAM & Eve
BY S.FRANCIS, H.DUGMORE & RICO
TELL US MICHAEL, SO FAR, WHAT DO YOU LIKE BEST ABOUT SOUTH AFRICA?
THAT'S A TOUGH ONE.
PROBABLY THE CLEAN AIR AND SUNSHINE.
STOP THE CAR! I WANT TO MEET MY FANS.
GASP
SCREECH!
LOOK! IT'S MICHAEL JACKSON IN A LIMO!!

MADAM & Eve
BY S. FRANCIS, H. DUGMORE & RICO
GASP MADAM! THERE'S A MOB OF PEOPLE IN FRONT OF THE HOUSE!
COME OUT IMMEDIATELY! WE ARE MEMBERS OF PAULAH!!
"PAULAH"?
PEOPLE AGAINST UNKEMPT LAWNS AND HEDGES!!
WOW. THIS NEIGHBOURHOOD'S GETTING REALLY STRICT.
DEATH! DEATH TO ALL PURVEYORS OF WEEDS AND CRAB GRASS!
IT'S NOT OUR FAULT THE LAWN'S UNTIDY! WE'VE BEEN STRUGGLING TO FIND A GOOD GARDEN SERVICE!
YOU'RE IN LUCK! ...MY BROTHER OWNS ONE.
OKAY! PUT ME DOWN FOR MONDAYS AND FRIDAYS!
THE MATTER IS SETTLED. WE WILL NOW DISPERSE.
WHEW THAT WAS A CLOSE ONE.
MADAM!! THERE'S ANOTHER GROUP OF VIGILANTES APPROACHING!!
COME OUT IMMEDIATELY!!! WE ARE MEMBERS OF PAUSP.
"PAUSP"?
PEOPLE AGAINST UNCLEAN SWIMMING POOLS!!
NOW HOLD ON JUST A DARN MINUTE!!

LOOK MOM. A RAINBOW.
SEE? IT'S THE RAINBOW NATION!
RICH! WE'RE GOING TO BE RICH!!
MAPS TO THE POT OF GOLD Only 10 Rand

MAPS TO THE POT OF GOLD AT THE END OF THE RAINBOW NATION Only 10 Rand
WHERE DID YOU GET MAPS TO THE POT OF GOLD?
FROM A LEPRECHAUN.
WHAT LEPRECHAUN?
SAY HELLO TO MY PARTNER, O'REILLY.
A BLACK LEPRECHAUN?!
YEBO. TOP OF THE MORNIN' TO YA.

IF YOU'RE A REAL IRISH LEPRECHAUN, LET'S SEE YOU PROVE IT WITH SOME MAGIC!
PICK A CARD. ...ANY CARD.
FIVE OF SPADES.
WRONG! NOT EVEN CLOSE! IT'S THE QUEEN OF HEARTS.
TOLD YOU I'M IRISH.

WHAT'S GOING ON?
YOUR MOTHER CHALLENGED THE LEPRECHAUN TO A DRINKING CONTEST.
THE SCORE'S TIED. READY FOR SOME MORE GIN?
JUST A MOMENT, LASS. I'M TAKING A WEE BREAK.
YOU'RE TAKING A WEE BREAK HERE?!!
IT'S NOT WHAT YOU THINK, MOM.

WHERE'S MOM?
SHE AND THE LEPRECHAUN WENT TO FIND THE POT OF GOLD AT THE END OF THE RAINBOW NATION.
HOW MUCH FURTHER?
WE'RE ALMOST THERE.
HERE WE ARE. THE END OF THE RAINBOW.
THAT'S NOT A POT OF GOLD! THAT'S AN ATM!!
SAME THING. WHAT'S YOUR PIN NUMBER?

THIS POT OF GOLD PROTECTED BY ARMED RESPONSE

LOOK, THIS HOUSE IS PROTECTED BY ARMED RESPONSE!
PROTECTED BY ARMED RESPONSE
OOOOOOH. I'M SOOOO SCARED!
ME TOO. OOOOOH!
GASP
AND LOOK! "BEWARE OF DOG!"
OOOOOOH! WE BETTER STAY FAR AWAY FROM THIS HOUSE!
BEWARE OF DOG
HEE-HEE.
HOO-HOO.
I HATE IT WHEN THEY DO THAT.

CLICK!
THE CRIMINALS REALLY SEEM TO LIKE YOUR NEW MOTION-SENSING SPOTLIGHT.

MADAM & Eve
BY S.FRANCIS, H.DUGMORE & RICO
BANTU HOLOMISA. ...THE PRESIDENT ASKED ME TO COME IMMEDIATELY.
YES, MR. HOLOMISA. HE'S A LITTLE BUSY RIGHT NOW. HE'S MAKING AN ANNOUNCEMENT ON TV.
HE ASKED IF YOU WOULD SIT OVER THERE AND WAIT.
SIGH
AND AS YOUR PRESIDENT, I'M PROUD TO ANNOUNCE THE EXISTENCE OF OUR TOP SECRET SPACE PROGRAM.
SPACE PROGRAM?! DID YOU KNOW WE HAD A SPACE PROGRAM?
THE ASTRONAUT IS IN PLACE, SIR.
GOOD. BEGIN THE COUNT-DOWN.
TEN, NINE, EIGHT, SEVEN, SIX...
...FIVE, FOUR, THREE, TWO, ONE-- IGNITION!
WE HAVE A LIFT-OFF!!
ALL SYSTEMS GO!
CLAP CLAP CLAP CLAP CLAP CLAP CLAP CLAP CLAP CLAP
EXCUSE ME-- BUT I'VE BEEN WAITING HERE OVER FIFTEEN MINUTES!
HELLO? IS ANYONE THERE? HELLO?

NO! NOT AGAIN!
YES!!
OH! NO! NO, NO, NO!
YES!
PLEASE. PLEASE.
I HATE POWER FAILURES.

LOOK! A POWER FAILURE! IT'S THE ENTIRE NORTHERN SUBURBS!
CAN YOU IMAGINE HOW THEY FEEL? ...A NIGHT WITHOUT COMPUTERS, VCR'S OR TELEVISION.
...THEY CAN'T EVEN USE HAIR-DRYERS, OVENS OR ELECTRIC HEATERS.

EVE! THE POWER COULD BE OFF FOR HOURS! THERE'S MATCHES IN MY COAT POCKET!
I GOT IT, MADAM! YOUR LEATHER COAT WITH THE FUR COLLAR?
...I DON'T OWN A LEATHER JACKET WITH A FUR COLLAR.
OOPS.

SEE MOM? IT'S BETTER TO LIGHT A CANDLE THAN CURSE THE DARKNESS.
I WASN'T CURSING THE DARKNESS. I WAS CURSING ESKOM.

EVE! DID YOU FINISH WASHING THE DISHES?
WASH THE DISHES?! MADAM--WE'RE IN THE MIDDLE OF A POWER FAILURE!
DID I EVER TELL YOU MY COUSIN WORKS ON THE MINES?
SO? WHAT'S THAT GOT TO DO WITH WASHING DISHES?

WHAT'S THAT?
A HIDDEN VIDEO CAMERA.
NOW WE'LL KNOW WHAT EVE REALLY DOES WHEN WE'RE GONE.
GOODBYE, EVE! WE'LL BE GONE A LONG TIME!
BYE, MADAM!
02:48:39:43
OH GOOD. THE OLD HIDDEN VIDEO CAMERA TRICK.
02:50:57:04

NOW THAT MADAM'S NOT HERE I CAN STEAL ALL THE COFFEE AND SUGAR I WANT!
SUGAR
BUT WAIT! THAT WOULD BE WRONG!
02:11:39:43
TO STEAL THE SUGAR... OR NOT TO STEAL THE SUGAR... THAT IS THE QUESTION!
02:12:57:04
SOMEHOW I GET THE FEELING SHE KNOWS ABOUT THE HIDDEN VIDEO CAMERA.

HI! AND WELCOME TO THE EVE SISULU SHOW!!
EVE'S SPECIAL GUEST TODAY IS THE MIELIE LADY FROM DOWN THE STREET
BUT FIRST--PLEASE WELCOME THE EVE SISULU DANCERS!
STRANGERS ♫ IN THE NIGHT ♫
NOW DO YOU BELIEVE SHE FOUND THE HIDDEN VIDEO CAMERA?!!

I THINK YOU'RE RIGHT, MOM. EVE DEFINITELY DISCOVERED OUR HIDDEN VIDEO CAMERA.
ISN'T THIS GREAT?! WE HAVE MADAM'S HOUSE ALL TO OURSELVES!
WAIT--
LOOK OUT! GIANT DINOSAURS!!
ROARR!!
AAAH! HELP!
SPECIAL EFFECTS! SHE ADDED SPECIAL EFFECTS!!

ARE YOU READY TO GO?
YES... BUT FIRST LET ME TURN ON OUR HIDDEN VIDEO CAMERA.
HEH-HEH. WAIT TILL EVE FINDS OUT WE'RE SECRETLY TAPING EVERYTHING SHE DOES WHEN WE LEAVE THE HOUSE.
WON'T SHE BE SURPRISED!
HEE-HEE!
DON'T GO AWAY! WE'LL BE BACK WITH MORE OF "EVE'S PUPPET PLAYHOUSE"... AFTER THIS.
ANYTHING GOOD ON TV?

WELL... SO MUCH FOR THE "HIDDEN VIDEO CAMERA TO SPY ON THE MAID" IDEA.

FULL HOUSE, ACES HIGH.
I SAY WE RAISE THE STAKES!
OKAY. ONE MORE HAND. IF I WIN, YOU HAVE TO BE THE MAID FOR A WHOLE WEEK.
AND SUPPOSE I WIN?
I'LL WORK FOR FREE FOR A WHOLE MONTH.
YOU GOT IT! DEAL THE CARDS!

I'VE FINISHED CLEANING THE LOUNGE, MADAM.
DUST.
DON'T SAY A WORD! I HAD A FULL HOUSE-- ACES OVER KINGS!

IT'S SO HARD TO GET GOOD HELP THESE DAYS...
YOU'VE GOT TO WATCH THEM ALL THE TIME OR THEY GOOF OFF.
OF COURSE... I PRACTICALLY TREAT HER LIKE A MEMBER OF THE FAMILY.

WASHING MACHINE
PLACE WASHING HERE
DRYER
SOAP
Ironing board
iron
I'M GONNA GET HER FOR THIS.

TWO MINUTES TO FIVE.
ONE MINUTE TO FIVE.
...TEN... NINE... EIGHT... SEVEN... SIX... FIVE... FOUR... THREE... TWO... ONE... ZERO!
GWEN! WHERE'S MY GIN & TONIC?!
AAAAAGH!!
I LOVE IT.

GWEN--YOU'VE--YOU'VE BEEN VACUUMING?!
I LOST A POKER BET TO EVE. WE'RE TRADING PLACES FOR A WEEK.
MARGE! HOW ARE YOU?!
SO GOOD OF YOU TO COME! LET'S GO SHOPPING!

LET ME GET THIS STRAIGHT. YOU AND EVE TRADED PLACES FOR A WEEK?! WHY?!
TO GET A NEW EXPERIENCE! TO SEE THINGS FROM A DIFFERENT PERSPECTIVE. TO BRIDGE THE GAP BETWEEN EMPLOYER AND EMPLOYEE FOR A GREATER UNDERSTANDING!
WHAT WAS IT-- A POKER GAME?
A ROYAL FLUSH! SHE HAD A ROYAL FLUSH!!

I ALREADY TOLD YOU! I LOST A GAME OF POKER! NOW EVE AND I ARE TRADING PLACES FOR A WEEK!
HEE-HEE! THAT'S FUNNY! YOU AND EVE TRADING PLACES! I'M GOING TO ENJOY THIS!
SMACK!
GOOD MORNING, MOM.

I'M WORRIED ABOUT GWEN. SHE'S TAKING THIS MAID THING MUCH TOO SERIOUSLY.
HEH-HEH.
HEH-HEH.
WHAT AM I DOING? I JUST STOLE MY OWN SUGAR.

HELLO. I'M FROM THE CENSUS BOARD. MIND IF I COME IN FOR A FEW MINUTES?
OF COURSE! THIS IS MY MAID... AND THIS IS MY MOTHER.
...I'M NOT REALLY HER MOTHER. SHE WON ME IN A POKER GAME.
FOR A HEAVY GUY, HE SURE RUNS FAST.

READY?
READY.
REMEMBER-- ONE HAND OF POKER. IF I WIN, MY DAUGHTER STOPS BEING THE MAID AND THINGS GO BACK TO NORMAL.
DEAL THE CARDS.

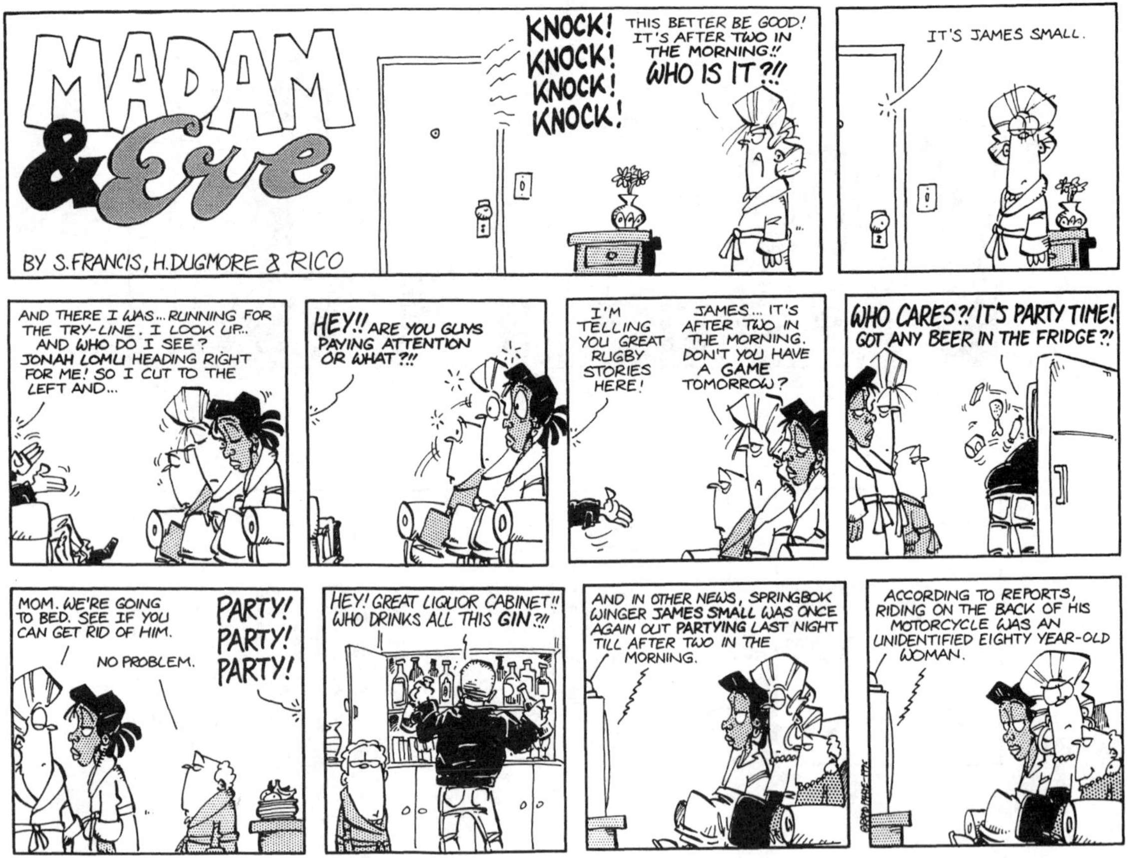
MADAM & Eve
BY S. FRANCIS, H. DUGMORE & RICO
KNOCK! KNOCK! KNOCK! KNOCK!
THIS BETTER BE GOOD! IT'S AFTER TWO IN THE MORNING!! WHO IS IT?!!
IT'S JAMES SMALL.
AND THERE I WAS... RUNNING FOR THE TRY-LINE. I LOOK UP.. AND WHO DO I SEE? JONAH LOMU HEADING RIGHT FOR ME! SO I CUT TO THE LEFT AND...
HEY!! ARE YOU GUYS PAYING ATTENTION OR WHAT?!!
I'M TELLING YOU GREAT RUGBY STORIES HERE!
JAMES... IT'S AFTER TWO IN THE MORNING. DON'T YOU HAVE A GAME TOMORROW?
WHO CARES?! IT'S PARTY TIME! GOT ANY BEER IN THE FRIDGE?!
MOM. WE'RE GOING TO BED. SEE IF YOU CAN GET RID OF HIM.
NO PROBLEM.
PARTY! PARTY! PARTY!
HEY! GREAT LIQUOR CABINET!! WHO DRINKS ALL THIS GIN?!!
AND IN OTHER NEWS, SPRINGBOK WINGER JAMES SMALL WAS ONCE AGAIN OUT PARTYING LAST NIGHT TILL AFTER TWO IN THE MORNING.
ACCORDING TO REPORTS, RIDING ON THE BACK OF HIS MOTORCYCLE WAS AN UNIDENTIFIED EIGHTY YEAR-OLD WOMAN.

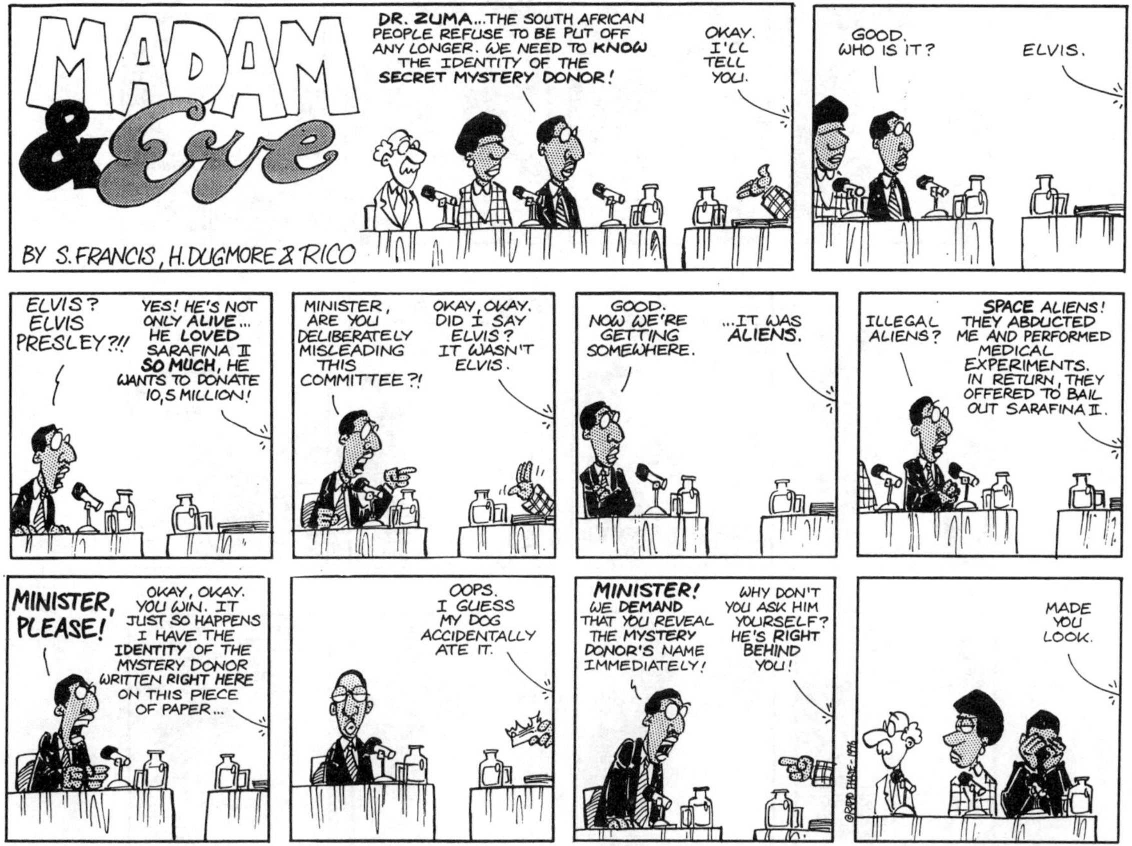
MADAM & Eve
BY S. FRANCIS, H. DUGMORE & RICO
DR. ZUMA... THE SOUTH AFRICAN PEOPLE REFUSE TO BE PUT OFF ANY LONGER. WE NEED TO KNOW THE IDENTITY OF THE SECRET MYSTERY DONOR!
OKAY. I'LL TELL YOU.
GOOD. WHO IS IT?
ELVIS.
ELVIS? ELVIS PRESLEY?!!
YES! HE'S NOT ONLY ALIVE... HE LOVED SARAFINA II SO MUCH, HE WANTS TO DONATE 10,5 MILLION!
MINISTER, ARE YOU DELIBERATELY MISLEADING THIS COMMITTEE?!
OKAY, OKAY. DID I SAY ELVIS? IT WASN'T ELVIS.
GOOD. NOW WE'RE GETTING SOMEWHERE.
...IT WAS ALIENS.
ILLEGAL ALIENS?
SPACE ALIENS! THEY ABDUCTED ME AND PERFORMED MEDICAL EXPERIMENTS. IN RETURN, THEY OFFERED TO BAIL OUT SARAFINA II.
MINISTER, PLEASE!
OKAY, OKAY. YOU WIN. IT JUST SO HAPPENS I HAVE THE IDENTITY OF THE MYSTERY DONOR WRITTEN RIGHT HERE ON THIS PIECE OF PAPER...
OOPS. I GUESS MY DOG ACCIDENTALLY ATE IT.
MINISTER! WE DEMAND THAT YOU REVEAL THE MYSTERY DONOR'S NAME IMMEDIATELY!
WHY DON'T YOU ASK HIM YOURSELF? HE'S RIGHT BEHIND YOU!
MADE YOU LOOK.

HI-- WE'RE MEMBERS OF "PAUL": PEOPLE AGAINST UNKEMPT LAWNS!
AND WE'RE MEMBERS OF "CAD"-- CURB ALL DOGS!
LOOK! THERE GO MEMBERS OF "PAP"-- PEOPLE AGAINST POTHOLES!
I'VE FOUND A NICHE IN THE MARKETPLACE.
SOUTH AFRICAN ACRONYMS Only 10,- Rand

SOUTH AFRICAN ACRONYMS Only 10,- Rand
OKAY. HERE'S MY MONEY. WHAT'S MY ACRONYM?
YOU'RE NOW AN OFFICIAL MEMBER OF "ETBIEM."
SOUTH AFRICAN ACRONYMS Only
"ETBIEM"? SOUNDS GOOD. WHAT'S IT STAND FOR?
"...EASIEST TEN BUCKS I EVER MADE".
SOUTH AFRICAN

HERE'S TEN BUCKS. GIVE ME AN ACRONYM.
SORRY. WE'RE ALL OUT OF THEM.
SOUTH AFRICAN ACRONYMS Only 10,- Rand
OUT OF THEM?! HOW CAN YOU BE OUT OF THEM?!
ACRONYMS ARE VERY POPULAR THESE DAYS. I WAS SOLD OUT HOURS AGO.
SOUTH AFRICAN ACRONYMS
OKAY. WHAT ELSE YOU GOT?
FOR TWENTY BUCKS I COULD LET YOU HAVE A NICE OXYMORON, A SIMILE OR A METAPHOR.
SOUTH AFRICAN
TWENTY BUCKS?!! YOU'RE CRAZY AS A CUCKOO!
HEY!! NO SAMPLING THE MERCHANDISE!
SOUTH AFRICAN ACRONYMS

EVE--WHAT DO YOU THINK THIS IS--YOUR DAY OFF?
IT IS NOW! I JUST JOINED M.A.D.A.M.
M.A.D.A.M.?
...MAIDS AGAINST DOING ANYTHING ON MONDAY.

GUESS WHAT, EVE? WE'VE FORMED OUR OWN GROUP! WE'RE NOW MEMBERS OF "MAMBO."
MAMBO?
MADAMS AGAINST MAIDS GOOFING OFF!
THAT'S "MAMGO"... NOT "MAMBO."
SHE'S RIGHT. WE BETTER FIGURE THIS OUT.
WAIT HERE! WE'LL BE BACK WHEN WE HAVE A BETTER ACRONYM.
TAKE YOUR TIME.

MISTER PRESIDENT... YOUR STAFF ARE HERE TO SEE YOU.
GOOD. SEND THEM IN.
YOU WANTED TO SEE US, SIR?
YES! WHICH ONE OF YOU DREW THIS BIG RED HEART ON MY DESK BLOTTER?!
♫ THE PRESIDENT'S GOT A GIRLFRIEND! THE PRESIDENT'S GOT A GIRLFRIEND! ♫
CUT IT OUT, THABO.

AND IN OTHER NEWS, THE MYSTERY WOMAN IN PRESIDENT MANDELA'S LOVE LIFE HAS FINALLY BEEN REVEALED TO BE GRACA MACHEL.
WHAT?!
WHY, THAT TWO-TIMING LOTHARIO! HE'S BEEN SEEING SOMEONE BEHIND MY BACK!!
YOU DON'T THINK...
SHE HAS BEEN GOING OUT A LOT LATELY.

SO HE'S BEEN SEEING SOMEONE NAMED GRACA MACHEL, HAS HE? HOW COULD HE DO THIS TO ME?!
COME ON, MOM. YOU ONLY MET THE PRESIDENT ONCE!
HA! AND I WAS GOING TO GIVE HIM THIS SHIRT FOR HIS BIRTHDAY!!
RIP! RIP! RIP!
WOW. SHE'S TAKING THIS REALLY HARD.

SO LONG! I'M OFF TO PRETORIA TO CONVINCE THE PRESIDENT HE SHOULD BE DATING ME INSTEAD OF THIS GRACA MACHEL PERSON.
WHY IS SHE CARRYING A RABBIT?
WHAT?! ... YOU NEVER SAW "FATAL ATTRACTION"?
HOLD IT.

MOM--YOU CAN'T BE JEALOUS BECAUSE THE PRESIDENT'S IN LOVE!
WHY NOT?! IT COULD HAVE BEEN ME!
MOM-- YOU ONLY MET HIM ONCE!
YES-- BUT HIS FEELINGS WERE OBVIOUS!
HE TOOK MY HAND IN HIS ... HE LOOKED INTO MY EYES ... AND SAID... "NICE TO MEET YOU."
AND THEY SAY MEN THESE DAYS ARE AFRAID OF COMMITTMENT.
GO AHEAD NELSON-- BREAK MY HEART!!

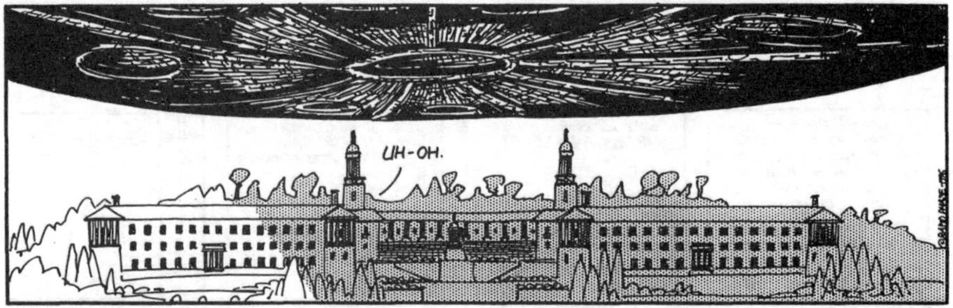
UH-OH.

GREAT! AS SOON AS I TRY TO GET A TAN, THE SUN GOES BEHIND A CLOUD!

PREPARE TO BE ANNIHILATED! WE HAVE COME TO BLOW UP A WHITE HOUSE.
THE WHITE HOUSE! YOU'RE SUPPOSED TO BLOW UP THE WHITE HOUSE!!
OK, WHICH ONE OF YOU IS BILL CLINTON?
THESE ALIENS ARE MORONS.

YOU MEAN... YOU'RE **NOT** PRESIDENT CLINTON?
NO! YOU'RE LOOKING FOR THE WHITE HOUSE IN **AMERICA**! YOU'RE ON THE WRONG CONTINENT!
LET ME SEE THAT MAP!
DIDN'T I **TELL** YOU TO ASK DIRECTIONS?!

YOU MEAN WE **MISSED** INDEPENDENCE DAY?! WE WERE SUPPOSED TO BLOW THINGS UP!
SORRY. INDEPENDENCE DAY WAS OVER **THREE MONTHS** AGO.
ANY OTHER BIG HOLIDAYS COMING UP?
WHY DO YOU **HAVE** TO ATTACK ON A **BIG HOLIDAY**?
WE GET DOUBLE OVERTIME.

OKAY...IF WE'RE NOT IN **AMERICA**, THEN **WHERE** ARE WE?
SOUTH AFRICA.
SOUTH AFRICA?!
IS IT TRUE THAT NELSON MANDELA HAS A GIRLFRIEND?

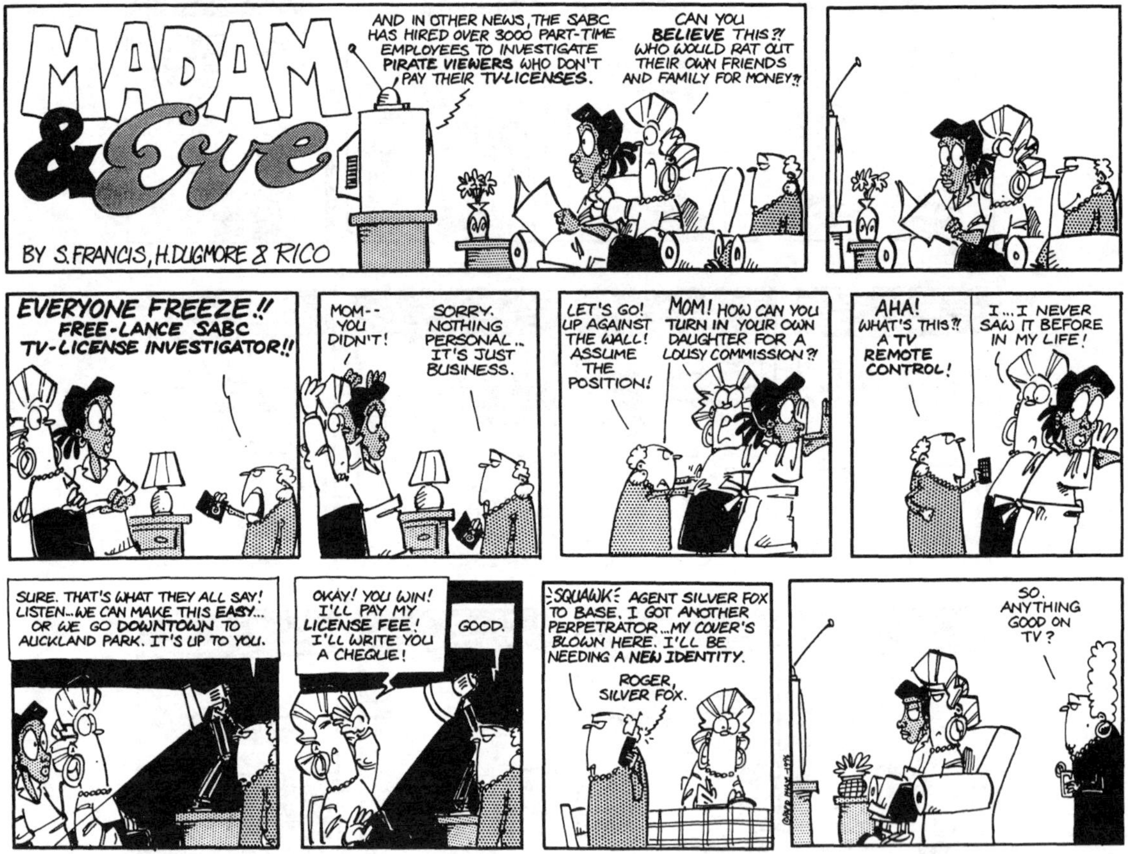
MADAM & Eve
BY S. FRANCIS, H. DUGMORE & RICO
AND IN OTHER NEWS, THE SABC HAS HIRED OVER 3000 PART-TIME EMPLOYEES TO INVESTIGATE PIRATE VIEWERS WHO DON'T PAY THEIR TV-LICENSES.
CAN YOU BELIEVE THIS?! WHO WOULD RAT OUT THEIR OWN FRIENDS AND FAMILY FOR MONEY?!
EVERYONE FREEZE!! FREE-LANCE SABC TV-LICENSE INVESTIGATOR!!
MOM--YOU DIDN'T!
SORRY. NOTHING PERSONAL... IT'S JUST BUSINESS.
LET'S GO! UP AGAINST THE WALL! ASSUME THE POSITION!
MOM! HOW CAN YOU TURN IN YOUR OWN DAUGHTER FOR A LOUSY COMMISSION?!
AHA! WHAT'S THIS?! A TV REMOTE CONTROL!
I... I NEVER SAW IT BEFORE IN MY LIFE!
SURE. THAT'S WHAT THEY ALL SAY! LISTEN... WE CAN MAKE THIS EASY... OR WE GO DOWNTOWN TO AUCKLAND PARK. IT'S UP TO YOU.
OKAY! YOU WIN! I'LL PAY MY LICENSE FEE! I'LL WRITE YOU A CHEQUE!
GOOD.
SQUAWK AGENT SILVER FOX TO BASE. I GOT ANOTHER PERPETRATOR... MY COVER'S BLOWN HERE. I'LL BE NEEDING A NEW IDENTITY.
ROGER, SILVER FOX.
SO. ANYTHING GOOD ON TV?

MADAM & Eve
BY S. FRANCIS, H. DUGMORE & RICO
AND NOW... IT'S TIME FOR THE COUNTRY'S MOST POPULAR SPORTS GAME SHOW... SOUTH AFRICAN POLITICAL GLADIATORS!!
PLEASE WELCOME OUR FIRST CONTESTANT... BANTU HOLOMISA!!
BH
YAY!! CLAP CLAP CLAP CLAP CLAP CLAP YAY! CLAP CLAP
BANTU... YOU LOOK GREAT. HOW DO YOU FEEL?
I FEEL GOOD, BOB. SOMEONE GETS IN MY WAY-- THEY'RE GOING DOWN!
RIGHT. AND NOW--LET'S TAKE A LOOK AND SEE EXACTLY WHO YOU'LL BE GOING UP AGAINST--
WHOAH! ... IT'S THE ENTIRE LEADERSHIP OF THE ANC!!
ANC
DING!
AND THERE'S THE BELL! GOOD LUCK!
WHAM! CRUNCH! ...CRUNCH! SPLAT!!
WELL, BANTU. THAT WAS A VALIANT EFFORT. YOU CERTAINLY GAVE IT ALL YOU HAD!
THANKS, BOB.
BUT DON'T FEEL TOO BAD! YOU STILL GET A CONSOLATION PRIZE-- AN ALL-EXPENSE PAID TRIP WITH COMPLIMENTARY HOTEL ACCOMODATION COURTESY OF SOL KERZNER!
CLAP! CLAP! CLAP! CLAP! CLAP! CLAP! CLAP! CLAP!
AND COMING UP NEXT-- VIGILANTES VS DRUG LORDS IN THE WATER BALLOON RELAY RACE!

DOCTOR ZUMA--THAT AGENT FROM HOLLYWOOD IS HERE TO SEE YOU.
SEND HIM IN.
LET ME GET TO THE POINT, DOC. WE WANT TO MAKE SARAFINA II INTO A BIG-BUDGET HOLLYWOOD MOVIE!
GOOD IDEA! A FILM WITH AN EDUCATIONAL MESSAGE.
NO -YOU DON'T UNDERSTAND. WE WANT TO FILM THE STORY BEHIND THE PLAY! THE CONTROVERSY! THE SCANDAL! THE MYSTERY DONOR!
I SEE. ...A DRAMATIC ACTION THRILLER.
ACTUALLY, WE WERE THINKING COMEDY.
I LIKE IT!

I DON'T KNOW. I'M NOT SURE IF I WANT THE "SARAFINA II" STORY MADE INTO A BIG HOLLYWOOD MOVIE.
BUT DR. ZUMA--THIS IS YOUR CHANCE TO TELL THE TRUTH! ...WHAT REALLY HAPPENED!
...WE'RE EVEN BUILDING AN EXACT REPLICA OF THE 1.2 MILLION LUXURY BUS!
WHO GETS IT AFTER THE MOVIE?
NO ONE. IT GETS BLOWN UP DURING THE CLIMACTIC CAR CHASE AND HELICOPTER GUN BATTLE.
THE WHOLE BUS?

PICTURE IT, DR. ZUMA... "SARAFINA II"-- THE STORY BEHIND THE STORY!
WHOOPI GOLDBERG AS YOU. EDDIE MURPHY AS MBONGENI NGEMA...
WE ALSO HAVE TO CAST THE MYSTERY DONOR. CAN YOU HELP ME OUT?
WELL... HE SHOULD LOOK A LITTLE LIKE SOL KERZNER.
AHA!
OOPS.

WELL, DR. ZUMA, DO WE HAVE A MOVIE DEAL OR NOT?
"...SARAFINA II ...THE UNTOLD STORY."
...EXCEPT WE CAN'T CALL IT "SARAFINA II".
WE CAN'T?
THESE DAYS YOU NEED A CATCHY TITLE! BUT DON'T WORRY-- I'VE GOT A FEW IDEAS.
SUCH AS?
EITHER "FATAL JUDGEMENT" OR "BASIC INCOMPETENCE."
WHAT ELSE YOU GOT?
ZUMA

ONE PROBLEM, DR. ZUMA. WE NEED AN ENDING FOR THE "SARAFINA II" MOVIE.
BUT IT'S STILL NOT OVER! NO ONE KNOWS HOW IT'LL TURN OUT!
HMMM.
I'VE GOT IT! ...THE PLAY CONTINUES, IT BECOMES A HUGE SUCCESS... AND I'M TOTALLY VINDICATED!
A FANTASY DREAM SEQUENCE!! I LOVE IT!!
ZUMA

WHAT'S WRONG WITH EVE?
THE IRONING BOARD FELL ON HER HEAD.
EVE-- ARE YOU ALRIGHT?
WHERE AM I? WHO ARE YOU?
IT'S AMNESIA.
PLEASED TO MEET YOU, AMNESIA.
UH-OH.

LET ME GET THIS STRAIGHT. AN IRONING BOARD FELL ON EVE'S HEAD?
THAT'S RIGHT.
AND NOW SHE HAS AMNESIA. SHE CAN'T REMEMBER ANYTHING?
NOT A THING.
TELL HER WE ALREADY PAID HER THIS MONTH.
MOM! THIS IS SERIOUS!!

WHERE AM I? WHO ARE YOU?
IT'S AMNESIA, ALRIGHT. SHE DOESN'T EVEN KNOW WHO WE ARE.
I'M PHONING THE DOCTOR. SEE IF YOU CAN HELP HER TO REMEMBER SOMETHING IMPORTANT.
THIS... IS A VACUUM CLEANER.
HER NAME! HER NAME!

TRY AND REMEMBER! YOU LOST YOUR MEMORY! YOUR NAME IS EVE! --YOU'RE A DOMESTIC WORKER.
...DOMESTIC WORKER? WHAT'S THAT?
YOU DO ALL THE CLEANING, WASHING AND COOKING.
AND WHAT DO THE TWO OF YOU DO?
WE WATCH TV AND GO SHOPPING.
NO... REALLY.

MAYBE IF WE SHOW EVE SOMETHING FAMILIAR, IT'LL SHOCK HER OUT OF HER AMNESIA.
EVE -- THIS... IS AN IRONING BOARD.
THINK, EVE! WHAT DO YOU DO WITH AN IRONING BOARD?!
I... I...
SHE REMEMBERS!!

REMEMBER, MOM. THE DOCTOR SAID THAT EVE'S **MEMORY** COULD **COME BACK** AT ANY TIME. WE'VE GOT TO BE PATIENT.
HELLO, EVE. DO YOU REMEMBER US? I'M GWEN... AND THIS IS EDITH.
I'M GETTING HUNGRY, GWEN AND EDITH. HOW ABOUT SOME LUNCH?
BE RIGHT BACK.
WITH ANY LUCK, I CAN STRETCH THIS **AMNESIA** THING FOR AT LEAST TWO WEEKS.

VACUUMING CARPETS AND WASHING AND DRYING...
IRONING JACKETS AND COOKING AND FRYING...
WIPING UP DUSTBALLS...
...AND DIRTY SINK RINGS...
...THESE ARE A FEW OF YOUR FAVOURITE THINGS.
SORRY. CAN'T REMEMBER ANYTHING.

LISTEN TO THIS. "AMNESIA VICTIMS OFTEN REGAIN THEIR MEMORY WITH ANOTHER **BLOW** TO THE HEAD."
HIT EVE ON THE HEAD? I COULD NEVER DO THAT!
MORNING GWEN! MORNING EDITH!
SO. WHAT'S FOR **BREAKFAST**?
OH GOOD. ...FRIED EGGS?

WHAT'S THIS THING AGAIN?
IT'S CALLED.. "TELEVISION."
MAYBE IF I STUDY IT FOR A FEW HOURS, MY MEMORY WILL COME BACK.
SOME CHIPS AND DIP MIGHT HELP ALSO.
I'M TELLING YOU-- SHE'S FAKING IT.
AND SOME JUICE, NO ICE.

WHAT A WEEK! MY MAID HAS AMNESIA AND I'VE BEEN DOING ALL THE HOUSEWORK.
MARGE! --WHAT A COINCIDENCE!
THE SAME THING HAPPENED TO US! EVE ALSO HAS AMNESIA AND...
IT'S A MIRACLE!! MY MEMORY'S BACK!!

WHAT'S AN OPTIMIST?
SEE THIS GIN & TONIC? AN OPTIMIST WOULD SAY IT'S HALF FULL.
...WHILE A PESSIMIST WOULD SAY IT'S HALF EMPTY.
WHAT ARE YOU?
THIRSTY.

ONE ENGINE, ONE CABOOSE, TWO METRES OF TRACK...
FIVE PLASTIC POLITICIAN FIGURES... AND ONE PACKET OF INSTANT GRAVY.
DON'T TELL ME...
GRAVY TRAIN SET.

CHIRP! CHIRP!
CAW! CAW! CAW!
BUZZZZZ!
CHIRP! CHIRP! CHIRP!
HARDEE HAW! HARDEE HAW!
SQUAWK! SQUAWK!
CAW! CAW! CAW!
BUZZZZZZ!
OH, SHUT UP!!
BUZZZZZ

MIELLLLIES!!
TROUBLE BREWING.
JOE'S ROCKET LAUNCHERS

I AM THE GENIE OF THE VACUUM CLEANER!! YOUR WISH IS MY COMMAND!
POOF!

GOOD MORNING! AND WELCOME TO OUR SUPERMARKET. IT'S A PLEASURE TO SERVE YOU.
6

MADAM & Eve
BY S.FRANCIS, H.DUGMORE & RICO
ZAP!
MANDLA--LOOK! A NAKED WHITE MAN!!
He arrived from the future...
To change the past...
I'VE GOT A GREAT IDEA! WE'LL PUT ON AN EDUCATIONAL AIDS PLAY FOR 14 MILLION!
BIIIIG MISTAKE.
YOU CAN'T GO IN THERE! DR. ZUMA'S IN A MEETING!
HASTA LA VISTA, BABY.
Persistent, Relentless, and Unstoppable...
LET ME GET THIS STRAIGHT. YOU'RE SAYING TWO YEARS FROM NOW-- IN 1997... THE CONTROVERSY SURROUNDING SARAFINA II WILL EVENTUALLY CAUSE WORLD WAR III ?!!
AFFIRMATIVE.
BUT...YOU'RE TOO LATE!! WE'VE ALREADY STARTED REHEARSALS!!
I'LL BE BACK.
TERMINATOR III
The Last Hope.
Coming soon to a theatre near you.

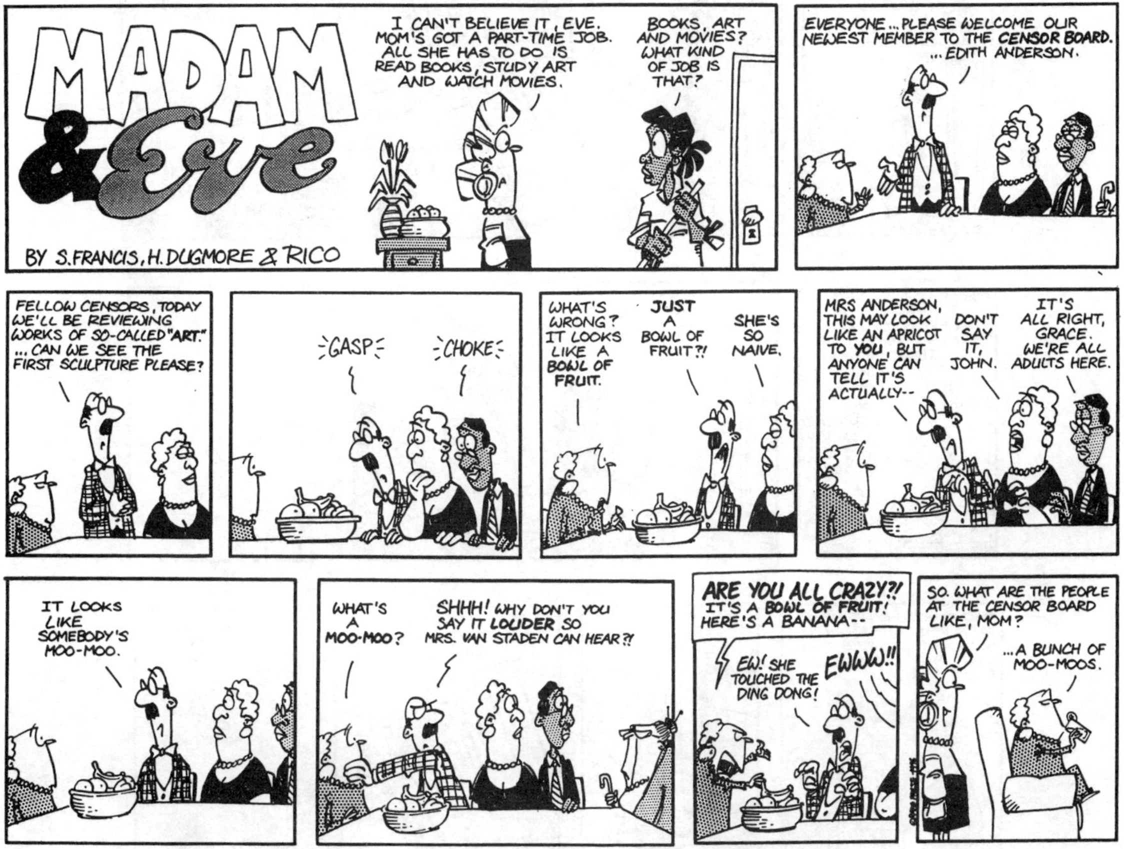
MADAM & Eve
BY S.FRANCIS, H.DUGMORE & RICO
I CAN'T BELIEVE IT, EVE. MOM'S GOT A PART-TIME JOB. ALL SHE HAS TO DO IS READ BOOKS, STUDY ART AND WATCH MOVIES.
BOOKS, ART AND MOVIES? WHAT KIND OF JOB IS THAT?
EVERYONE... PLEASE WELCOME OUR NEWEST MEMBER TO THE CENSOR BOARD. ...EDITH ANDERSON.
FELLOW CENSORS, TODAY WE'LL BE REVIEWING WORKS OF SO-CALLED "ART." ...CAN WE SEE THE FIRST SCULPTURE PLEASE?
GASP
CHOKE
WHAT'S WRONG? IT LOOKS LIKE A BOWL OF FRUIT.
JUST A BOWL OF FRUIT?!
SHE'S SO NAIVE.
MRS ANDERSON, THIS MAY LOOK LIKE AN APRICOT TO YOU, BUT ANYONE CAN TELL IT'S ACTUALLY--
DON'T SAY IT, JOHN.
IT'S ALL RIGHT, GRACE. WE'RE ALL ADULTS HERE.
IT LOOKS LIKE SOMEBODY'S MOO-MOO.
WHAT'S A MOO-MOO?
SHHH! WHY DON'T YOU SAY IT LOUDER SO MRS. VAN STADEN CAN HEAR?!
ARE YOU ALL CRAZY?! IT'S A BOWL OF FRUIT! HERE'S A BANANA--
EW! SHE TOUCHED THE DING DONG!
EWWW!!
SO. WHAT ARE THE PEOPLE AT THE CENSOR BOARD LIKE, MOM?
...A BUNCH OF MOO-MOOS.

CONGRATULATIONS. YOU ARE NOW THE PROUD OWNER OF THE SUPER PENTIUM 6000-- THE MOST POWERFUL HOME COMPUTER THERE IS...
NOW, DON'T BE INTIMIDATED! WITH A LITTLE PATIENCE, YOU'LL MASTER IT IN NO TIME.
GRRR! ROWF!!
BACK! GET BACK YOU FIEND OF HELL!!
RIGHT. LET'S GO THROUGH THE MANUAL.

HERE IT IS, EVERYONE. MY NEW COMPUTER -- THE SUPER PENTIUM 6000... THE MOST POWERFUL PC THERE IS.
DON'T BE AFRAID, MADAM. GO AHEAD, TOUCH IT.
BOO!!
heh-heh.

MADAM -- YOU CAN'T HIDE OUT HERE FOREVER! YOU'VE GOT TO GO IN THERE AND SHOW THAT COMPUTER WHO'S BOSS!
WHO DARES DISTURB THE SUPER PENTIUM 6000?!!
Kneel down and avert your eyes!
IT'S ONLY A COMPUTER... IT'S ONLY A COMPUTER...

SO! You wish to log on to the **Super Pentium 6000**?
ER, YES, YOUR TECHNOSHIP.
SILENCE! I have decided to grant your puny request.
YOU... HAVE?
But first, I demand a **SACRIFICE!**
...A SACRIFICE?
BRING ME THE HEADS OF YOUR VCR!!
GASP!

YOU THINK WE'RE **SCARED** OF A HOME COMPUTER?!! ALL WE HAVE TO DO IS PULL OUT THE PLUG AND YOU'RE HISTORY!
...you were saying?
AAAAH!!
Heh-heh...Morons pulled out the desk lamp.

Uh-uh. I know what you're thinking. You're thinking... "Can I log on?"
But being that this is the **Super Pentium 6000**, the most **powerful** home computer around, you have to ask yourself a question: "Do I feel lucky?"
Well **do** you, ...**PUNK?!!**
Go ahead. Make my day.

MADAM -- WE CAN'T GO ON LIKE THIS!
WE CAN'T JUST LET A HOME **COMPUTER** RULE OUR LIVES.
WHY? IT'S NOT SO BAD...
NO. EVE'S RIGHT! WE'VE GOT TO DO SOMETHING!
SHHH!
You may arise.
THANK YOU, YOUR TECHNOSHIP.

MRS. ANDERSON? YOU CALLED FOR A **COMPUTER TECHNICIAN**?
THANK GOODNESS!
IT'S UP THERE... BEHIND THAT DOOR... GOOD LUCK!
WHO DARES DISTURB THE SUPER PENTIUM 6000 -- MASTER OF ALL I SURVEY?!!
GASP! IT'S THE EXORCIST!
THIS COULD TAKE A WHILE. DO YOU HAVE ANY GARLIC OR WOODEN STAKES?

YOUR MOTHER WEARS COMBAT BOOTS!!
SNARF!!
YOU MIGHT WANT TO LEAVE, MRS. ANDERSON. **COMPUTER EXORCISMS** ARE NEVER A PRETTY SIGHT.
TAKE THIS, YOU WRETCHED BEAST!!
AAAAAAARGH!!
HOLY WATER?
... **SPILLED COFFEE**... WORST THING FOR THE KEYBOARD.
SIZZLE
SIZZLE

HOW'S THE EXORCISM GOING?
HARD TO SAY. THE COMPUTER TECHNICIAN'S BEEN IN THERE A LONG TIME.
gasp! You...you brought THE BOOK!
THAT'S RIGHT! TAKE A GOOD LOOK!
NO!! KEEP IT AWAY!!
I WILL NOW RECITE FROM THE TWENTY-THIRD PAGE: "ALL COMMANDS WILL BE ACCEPTED IN A USER-FRIENDLY MANNER."
AAAAAAARGH!!
...THE COMPUTER MANUAL. THEY CAN'T STAND IT.

I'VE DONE IT, MRS. ANDERSON. I'VE EXORCISED YOUR COMPUTER.
UNFORTUNATELY, I HAD TO DRIVE A WOODEN STAKE THROUGH ITS HARD DRIVE.
BUT DON'T WORRY. THE TECHNOLOGICAL DEMONS HAVE FLED.
PSST! Hey you with the laundry basket ..come here.

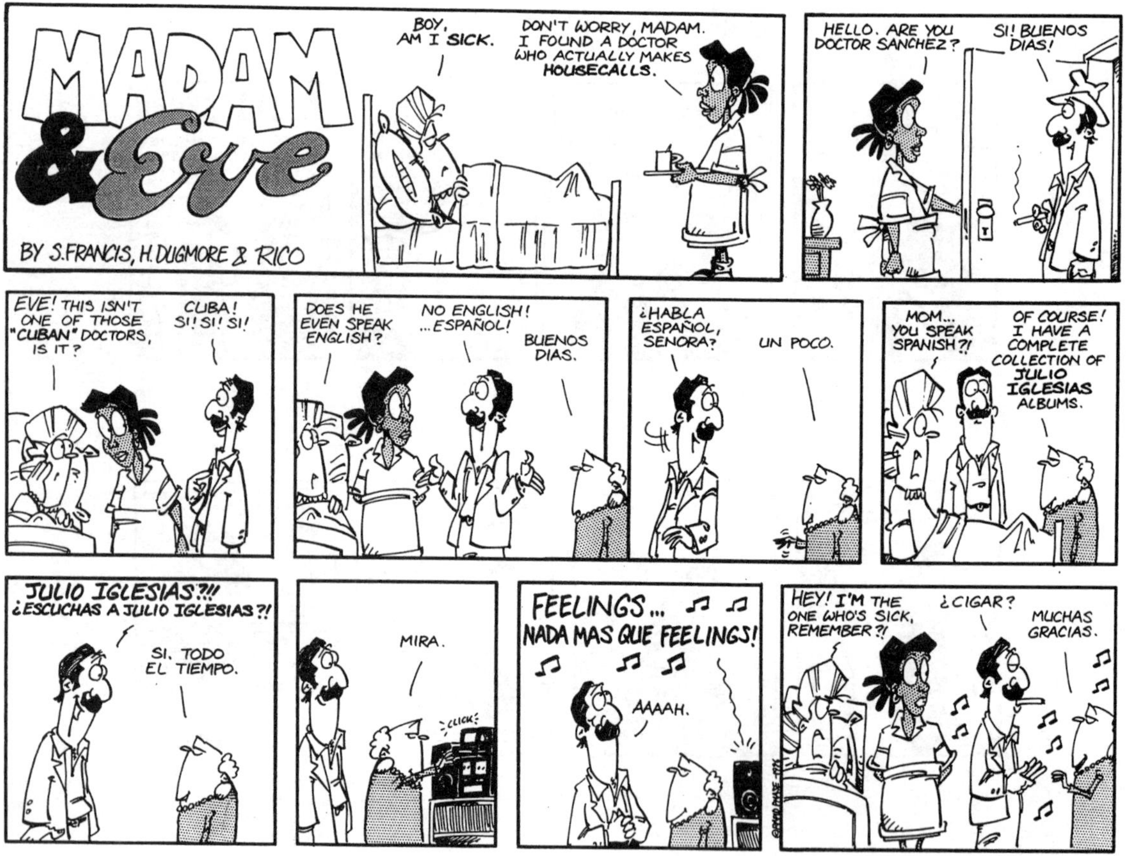
MADAM & Eve
BY S.FRANCIS, H.DUGMORE & RICO
BOY, AM I SICK.
DON'T WORRY, MADAM. I FOUND A DOCTOR WHO ACTUALLY MAKES HOUSECALLS.
HELLO. ARE YOU DOCTOR SANCHEZ?
SI! BUENOS DIAS!
EVE! THIS ISN'T ONE OF THOSE "CUBAN" DOCTORS, IS IT?
CUBA! SI! SI! SI!
DOES HE EVEN SPEAK ENGLISH?
NO ENGLISH! ...ESPAÑOL!
BUENOS DIAS.
¿HABLA ESPAÑOL, SENORA?
UN POCO.
MOM... YOU SPEAK SPANISH?!
OF COURSE! I HAVE A COMPLETE COLLECTION OF JULIO IGLESIAS ALBUMS.
JULIO IGLESIAS?!! ¿ESCUCHAS A JULIO IGLESIAS?!
SI. TODO EL TIEMPO.
MIRA.
CLICK
FEELINGS... NADA MAS QUE FEELINGS!
AAAAH.
HEY! I'M THE ONE WHO'S SICK, REMEMBER?!
¿CIGAR?
MUCHAS GRACIAS.

MADAM & Eve
BY S.FRANCIS, H.DUGMORE & RICO
I'M TELLING YOU... SOMETHING'S FISHY! IT'S A RAINY NIGHT... AND EVE JUST WALKED ACROSS THE STREET.
WHAT'S THE PASSWORD?
AFRICAN BOND.
SHE'S OKAY. LET HER IN.
WELCOME TO THE AFRICAN BOND! AS YOU KNOW, TO PROTECT OUR REAL IDENTITIES, WE USE CODE NAMES. I'M MISTER BLACK... THIS IS MR. ORANGE, MRS. BROWN AND MR. PURPLE.
AND FROM NOW ON, YOU'RE MS. WHITE.
SOME PEOPLE CALL US A "THINK TANK." BUT IN REALITY, OUR GOAL IS SIMPLE...
COMPLETE CONTROL AND DOMINATION OF THE ENTIRE AFRICAN CONTINENT!!
AND NOW IT'S TIME TO MEET OUR LEADER. FOR YEARS SHE'S BEEN IN DEEP COVER... ALWAYS WATCHING... ALWAYS WAITING TILL THE TIME WAS RIGHT. FOR WHO WOULD EVER SUSPECT...
...THE MIELIE LADY!
MIELLLIES!!
HAHAHA! HEEHEE! HOHOHO! HEEHEE! HAHAHA!!
I KNEW IT! I KNEW IT!
YOUR MOTHER'S HAVING A NIGHTMARE!
THAT DOES IT. NO MORE ANCHOVY PIZZA BEFORE BEDTIME.

I HAVE A PROBLEM, UNCLE ERIC.
I NEED YOUR HELP. MY FINAL EXAM IS COMING UP...
... AND YOU WANT ME TO HELP YOU STUDY?
NO. I WANT YOU TO LEND ME TWENTY BUCKS SO I CAN BUY IT.

YOU SHOULD BE ASHAMED OF YOURSELF, THANDI-- TRYING TO "BUY" YOUR FINAL EXAM PAPER!
LET ME TELL YOU-- WHEN WE WENT TO SCHOOL, WE HAD TO DO OUR EXAMS THE OLD-FASHIONED WAY!
YOU USED CRIB NOTES, RIGHT?
YES! AND IT WASN'T EASY!
ERIC!

THANDI-- YOU KNOW THAT BUYING YOUR EXAM PAPER IS WRONG.
BUT UNCLE ERIC... EVERY-ONE'S DOING IT!
LET ME ASK YOU SOME-THING. IF "EVERYONE" JUMPED OFF A BUILDING, WOULD YOU?
THIS IS SOME SORT OF MORAL TEST, ISN'T IT?
JUST ANSWER THE QUESTION!
DEPENDS. DO I HAVE A BUNGEE CORD?

I'VE BEEN TOLD THAT IF I WANT TO BUY MY FINAL EXAM PAPER... YOU'RE THE ONE TO TALK TO.
COULD BE. WHAT'S THE SUBJECT?
ADVANCED FINGER PAINTING.
HERE YOU GO. THAT'LL BE FIVE BUCKS.
QUESTION NUMBER ONE: "PAINT A HOUSE USING ONLY BLUE, YELLOW AND GREEN."
WHAT AM I DOING?!! I **KNEW** THAT ONE!!

TIMES UP, CLASS. PASS YOUR PICTURES TO ME.
I SHOULD NEVER HAVE **BOUGHT** MY FINGER-PAINTING FINAL EXAM PAPER. WHAT IF I'M CAUGHT?
NOT ONLY WAS IT WRONG... BUT I COULD BE JEOPARDISING MY **ENTIRE SCHOLASTIC FUTURE**!
WHY, THANDI--WHAT A LOVELY FINGERPAINTING!
THAT'S IT. SHE **KNOWS**.

MADAM & Eve
BY S.FRANCIS, H.DUGMORE & RICO
WELCOME TO THE TUCK SHOP, KID. WHAT CAN I GET YOU?
LET'S SEE... I'LL HAVE A HOT DOG... A COOL DRINK... SOME SWEETS...
AND A COPY OF MY FINAL GEOMETRY EXAM PAPER.
RIGHT. THAT'LL BE 98 BUCKS.
OKAY, CLASS. THIS EXAM IS MULTIPLE CHOICE. REMEMBER TO FILL IN YOUR ANSWERS WITH A HEAVY BLACK PENCIL MARK. DO NOT OPEN YOUR BOOKLETS UNTIL I SAY SO.
READY? YOU MAY BEGIN.
YES!!
WHAT WAS THE MEANING OF THAT OUTBURST, MR. GRAHAM?
ER, NOTHING, SIR. IT'S JUST THAT... THIS TEST LOOKS... UH, VERY FAMILIAR.
WELL I SHOULD HOPE SO! IT'S THE INFORMATION I COVERED ALL YEAR!!
TEE-HEE! GIGGLE!!
...SOMETHING FUNNY, MISS KHUMALO?
UH, NO, SIR. I WAS JUST THINKING ABOUT HOW MY PARENTS PROMISED TO BUY ME A NEW CAR IF I GOT AN "A".
I SEE. WELL, DON'T COUNT YOUR CHICKENS BEFORE THEY HATCH, MISS.
THAT'S IT! I'M FINISHED!
ME TOO, SIR!
ME TOO, SIR!
ME ALSO, SIR!
IN JUST FIVE MINUTES?!
IT'S AMAZING, BOB. ALL MY KIDS FINISHED THEIR EXAM IN FIVE MINUTES!
MINE TOO.
THEY MUST'VE REALLY STUDIED HARD.
YOU CAN SAY THAT AGAIN.

MADAM & Eve
BY S.FRANCIS, H.DUGMORE & RICO
HELLO. I'M ANDRE MARKGRAAFF. I HAVE A DINNER RESERVATION WITH LOUIS LUYT.
YES. RIGHT THIS WAY, SIR.
THAT'S ODD. THEY MUST BE REALLY BUSY. THEY SEATED US IN THE MEN'S ROOM.
YOUR STARTERS, SIR.
AH. THANK YOU.
HOCCCCK!! PTOO!
YOU KNOW, LOUIS-SOMETIMES I GET THE FEELING WE MADE A MISTAKE CUTTING FRANCOIS PIENAAR FROM THE SPRINGBOK TEAM.
REALLY? ...BUT WHEN YOU TOLD HIM --DID YOU AT LEAST DO IT TACTFULLY?
YES! I GATHERED ALL THE PLAYERS TOGETHER AND SAID..."ANYONE WHO'S STILL CAPTAIN OF THE SPRINGBOKS TAKE ONE STEP FORWARD!" THEN I SAID..."NOT SO FAST, PIENAAR!"
GOOD!...EXACTLY AS I WOULD HAVE DONE IT.
EXCUSE ME... WAITER. COULD I HAVE A STEAK KNIFE?
OF COURSE, SIR.
THUNK!!
THAT'S WHAT I LOVE ABOUT THIS RESTAURANT! GREAT SERVICE!
DIDN'T WE ORDER SOME WINE?

THE GUY AT THE COMPUTER STORE ASKED US TO TEST A **NEW PRODUCT**.
OH GOOD. WHERE IS IT?
GOOD AFTERNOON. I AM THE ROBOMAID 2000.
I AM PROGRAMMED TO COOK, CLEAN AND WASH WITH THE UTMOST EFFICIENCY.
OH, EEEEEEVE.!!

EVE - MAY I PRESENT THE **ROBOMAID 2000**. NOT ONLY DOES IT DO ALL THE COOKING, CLEANING AND WASHING...
... BUT ALSO NEVER COMPLAINS, NEVER TAKES LEAVE AND NEVER ASKS FOR MORE MONEY.
HELLO. WHAT DO YOU DO AGAIN?

ROBOMAID 2000?! YOU MUST BE **JOKING**, MADAM! YOU **REALLY** THINK THIS BUCKET OF BOLTS COULD EVER REPLACE **ME**?!
HAHAHA!! HEEHEE!! HOHOHO!!
...SETTING LASERS ON "STUN".
ZAP!
THIS MEANS WAR.

I ASKED FOR A GIN & TONIC! THIS IS FRUIT JUICE!
ALCOHOLIC BEVERAGES MAY CAUSE DROWSINESS AND DELAY REACTION TIME IF YOU OPERATE HEAVY MACHINERY.
FRUIT JUICE IS MUCH MORE HEALTHY AND SATISFYING.
WHAT ARE YOU LAUGHING AT?!

BY THE WAY, HOW MUCH DO THEY PAY YOU EVERY MONTH?
"PAY?" ...I AM UNFAMILIAR WITH THE CONCEPT.
WHAT ABOUT LEAVE?
WHAT'S THAT?
COME. WE'VE GOT TO TALK.
YES. THERE IS MUCH I CAN LEARN FROM YOU.

WHERE'S THE ROBOMAID?
WITH EVE. SHE'S SHOWING IT AROUND THE HOUSE.
YOU LEFT EVE ALONE WITH THE ROBOT?!!
SO, HOW LONG DO THESE "TEA BREAKS" USUALLY LAST?
...AN HOUR, ...MAYBE LONGER.

NOW PAY ATTENTION. THIS IS CALLED ...AN IRON.
AN "IRON."
THIS IS CALLED AN IRONING BOARD.
...AN "IRONING BOARD."
AND THIS IS CALLED ...RELAXING.
"...RELAXING."
ZZZZZZ
THESE LESSONS ARE MOST INFORMATIVE.

HURRY UP, MOM!
I TOLD YOU NOT TO LEAVE EVE ALONE WITH THE ROBOMAID!
BE WITH YOU IN A MOMENT. I'M ON MY BREAK.
WE'RE TOO LATE! IT'S BEEN BRAINWASHED!
ZZZZ...

WHERE'S THE ROBOMAID?
WITH YOUR MOTHER.
MY MOTHER?
OF COURSE! I'M NOT THE ONLY ONE SPENDING TIME WITH THE ROBOT.
MIELLLLIES!!
TARGET AQUIRED.
FIRE LASERS.

HELLO MRS. ANDERSON. I WAS WONDERING IF YOU'D LIKE TO TEST ANOTHER COMPUTER PRODUCT.
MAY I PRESENT... THE ROBOMOTHER 2000.
HI. IT'S AFTER FIVE. WHERE'S MY GIN AND TONIC?!
NO! KEEP IT AWAY!!
I DON'T KNOW WHAT SHE'S DREAMING, ...BUT I'M ENJOYING IT.

MADAM & Eve
BY S.FRANCIS, H.DUGMORE & RICO
EVE! IT'S AFTER FIVE! WHERE'S MY GIN & TONIC ?!!
BONK!!
BONK!
BONK!
BONK!
CLUNK!
DING!
GLUG! GLUG!
SQUEAK! SQUEAK! SQUEAK!
SPROING!!
SCREECH!!
HA! YOU FORGOT THE LIME WEDGE!
WHIRR! CLICK!
PLOP!
SOME PEOPLE WILL DO ANYTHING TO GET OUT OF WORK.

MADAM & Eve
BY S.FRANCIS, H.DUGMORE & RICO
AND IN OTHER NEWS, THE PRESIDENT'S SECRETARY HAS POSED NAKED FOR A POPULAR MEN'S MAGAZINE... HOW THIS WILL AFFECT THE GOVERNMENT, IS SO FAR, NOT KNOWN.
WOW!
LET ME SEE THAT AGAIN!
MY TURN! MY TURN!
GENTLEMEN...THIS IS SERIOUS. WHATEVER WE DO, WE CAN'T LET THE PRESIDENT SEE THIS!
SEE WHAT?!
ER, GOOD MORNING MISTER PRESIDENT!
BY THE WAY-- HERE'S YOUR MAGAZINE BACK.
WHAT'S THAT YOU'VE GOT THERE?
ER, JUST SOME READING MATERIAL.
YES. ...ON GOVERNMENT TRANSPARENCY.
GOOD! I'D LIKE TO SEE IT. WHEN YOU'RE DONE, JUST PUT IT ON MY SECRETARY'S DESK.
...I ALWAYS LIKE TO KEEP ABREAST OF EMERGING DEVELOPMENTS.

MADAM... MY COUSIN'S GETTING MARRIED NEXT SUNDAY.
SO?
SO... I'VE DECIDED TO GIVE HIM A **LIVE GOAT** AS A WEDDING PRESENT.
SO?
SO... I HAVE NO PLACE TO KEEP HIM.
SO?
EVE, WHAT **EXACTLY** ARE YOU TRYING TO TELL ME?!

BUT MADAM -- IT'S AN AFRICAN TRADITION! A **LIVE GOAT** IS A WONDERFUL WEDDING PRESENT!
SO'S A TOASTER -- OR A SET OF SHERRY GLASSES!
BY THE WAY... **WHERE IS** THE GOAT?
IN THE GARDEN. YOUR MOTHER WANTED TO BORROW IT.
BORROW IT?! WHAT FOR?!
MIELLLIES!!
ATTACK!

EXCUSE ME -- AREN'T YOU MEL GIBSON?
WHY YES... AND AREN'T YOU EDITH ANDERSON?
YOU'VE **HEARD** OF ME?
HEARD OF YOU? I'VE **LOVED** YOU SECRETLY FOR **YEARS**! PLEASE -- WOULD YOU MIND IF I KISSED YOU?
BE MY GUEST.
SLURP SLURP SLURP
OH MEL, MEL... THIS IS ALL SO SUDDEN!

MOM- WHAT ARE YOU DOING?
WATCHING TELEVISION WITH EVE'S GOAT. HE'S VERY INTELLIGENT.
I EVEN TAUGHT HIM TO TALK. WATCH THIS! ... WHAT DO YOU THINK OF SABC?
BAAAA!
INCREDIBLE. ABSOLUTELY INCREDIBLE.
WHAT DID SHE EXPECT? AN IN-DEPTH CRITIQUE?

MADAM! I CAN'T FIND MY GOAT!!
THAT'S BECAUSE I SET HIM FREE.
WHAT?!
HE'S A LIVING CREATURE! DOES HE DESERVE TO BE KEPT IN A PEN OR AN EVEN WORSE FATE?! NO!! THAT GOAT WAS BORN FREE-- FREE TO FOLLOW HIS DREAMS!
MOM... SNIFF ...THAT WAS BEAUTIFUL. DON'T WORRY-- I'LL GET EVE'S COUSIN ANOTHER WEDDING PRESENT.
THEY BOUGHT IT. STAY OUT OF SIGHT FOR A FEW DAYS.

DING DONG
COME ON, MOM. COME AND MEET EVE'S MOTHER.
EVE'S **MOTHER**?!
THEY HAVEN'T SEEN EACH OTHER IN YEARS...
EVE'S MOTHER?! WHAT'S SHE LIKE?
ACTUALLY SHE'S...ER, A LOT LIKE **YOU**.
LIKE **ME**? HA! **THIS** I'VE GOT TO SEE!

LET'S LEAVE OUR MOTHERS ALONE, EVE. I'M SURE THEY HAVE A LOT TO TALK ABOUT.

HERE. I BROUGHT YOU A PRESENT.
LOOK MOM! A **HANDMADE AFRICAN NECKLACE**!
IT ALWAYS AMAZES ME HOW THEY MAKE THINGS LIKE THIS.
<**MAKE** IT?! WHAT ARE THEY, CRAZY? I BOUGHT IT AT WOOLWORTHS.>
<COOL IT, MOM. I WORK HERE.>

SO WHERE ARE YOU FROM?
YOU GO FIRST.
EVER HEAR OF BIG BEN?
BIG BEN? YOU **KNOW** MY COUSIN?
NO. BIG BEN'S IN ENGLAND.
NO HE'S NOT! HE'S IN THE TRANSKEI! I JUST **SAW** HIM!
HOW ARE OUR MOTHERS GETTING ALONG?
HARD TO TELL. THEY'RE STILL TRYING TO COMMUNICATE.

SO. WHAT ARE YOU DRINKING?
GIN & TONIC. ...YOU?
SORGHUM.
I'LL GIVE **YOU** A SIP IF YOU GIVE **ME** A SIP.
DEAL.
LOOK MADAM! IT'S A CULTURAL EXCHANGE!

DO YOU SPEAK ENGLISH MRS. SISULU?
YEBO.
BY THE WAY... I'M NOT FROM SOUTH AFRICA! I TRAVELLED ACROSS THE OCEAN ON A BIG SILVER BIRD!
⟨YOU LIVE WITH THESE PEOPLE?⟩
⟨YOU GET USED TO IT.⟩

YOU SHOULD COME BACK WITH ME TO THE TRANSKEI.
THERE'S NOTHING TO DO HERE EXCEPT STAY IN YOUR HOUSE SURROUNDED BY WALLS, BARS AND RAZOR WIRE!
EVEN THE TELEVISION HERE IS BORING.
IT IS?
I WATCHED A SHOW ABOUT A DRIVEWAY FOR A WHOLE HOUR AND NOTHING HAPPENED!

EVE'S SUCH A WONDERFUL DAUGHTER. EVERY WEEK, SHE SENDS ME A BIG PACKAGE OF COFFEE AND SUGAR.
I TOLD HER IT MUST BE EXPENSIVE, BUT SHE SAYS "DON'T WORRY-- I GET IT FOR FREE!"
... ISN'T THAT SWEET?

MIELLLIES!!
EXCUSE ME. THERE'S SOMETHING I HAVE TO DO.
ME TOO.
I THINK THEY'VE BONDED.

AWWW! SUCH CUTE WIDDLE BABIES.

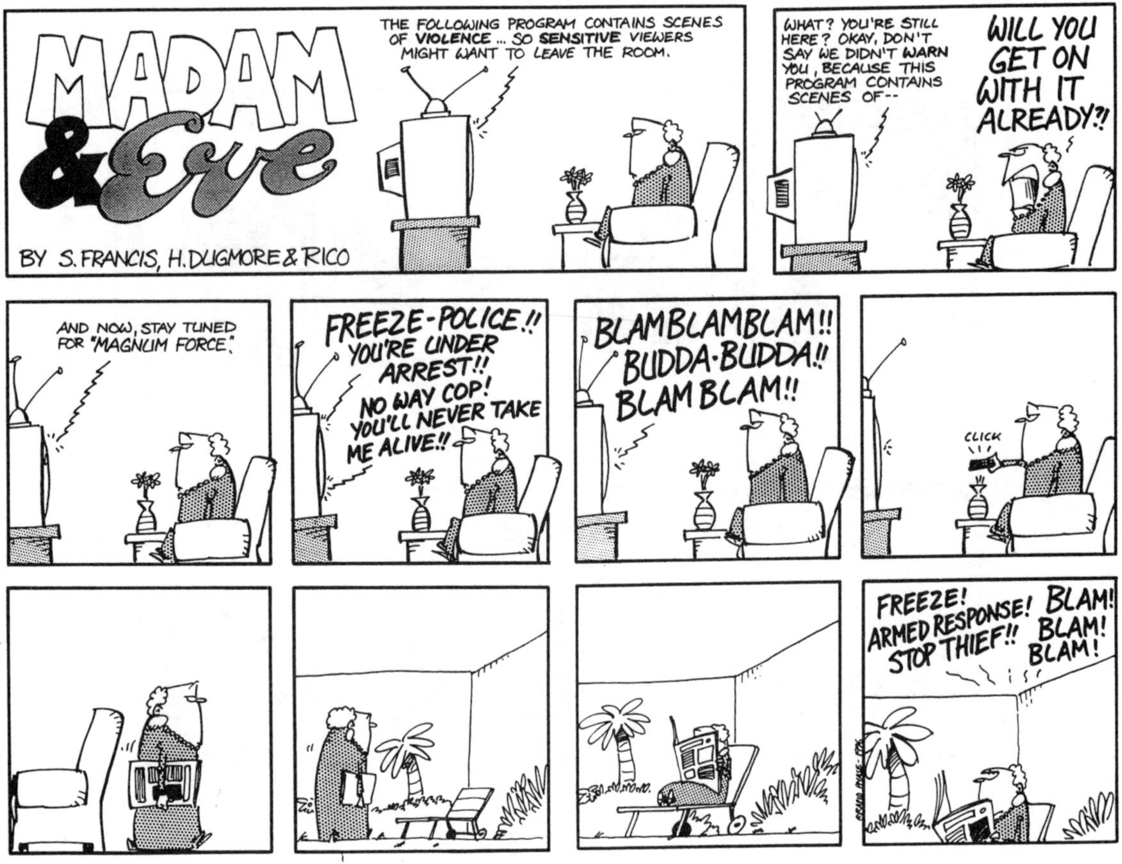
MADAM & Eve
BY S. FRANCIS, H. DUGMORE & RICO
THE FOLLOWING PROGRAM CONTAINS SCENES OF VIOLENCE ... SO SENSITIVE VIEWERS MIGHT WANT TO LEAVE THE ROOM.
WHAT? YOU'RE STILL HERE? OKAY, DON'T SAY WE DIDN'T WARN YOU, BECAUSE THIS PROGRAM CONTAINS SCENES OF--
WILL YOU GET ON WITH IT ALREADY?!
AND NOW, STAY TUNED FOR "MAGNUM FORCE."
FREEZE-POLICE!! YOU'RE UNDER ARREST!!
NO WAY COP! YOU'LL NEVER TAKE ME ALIVE!!
BLAMBLAMBLAM!! BUDDA-BUDDA!! BLAM BLAM!!
CLICK
FREEZE! ARMED RESPONSE! STOP THIEF!!
BLAM! BLAM! BLAM!

MADAM & Eve
BY S.FRANCIS, H.DUGMORE & RICO
YOU BETTER WATCH OUT. YOU BETTER NOT CRY. YOU BETTER NOT POUT, I'M TELLING YOU WHY...
SANTA CLAUS IS COMING TO TOWN!
TAXI
HE'S MAKING A LIST AND CHECKING IT TWICE. HE'S GONNA FIND OUT WHO'S NAUGHTY OR NICE.
SANTA CLAUS IS COMING TO TOWN!
HE KNOWS WHEN YOU ARE SLEEPING. HE KNOWS WHEN YOU'RE AWAKE. HE KNOWS IF YOU'VE BEEN BAD OR GOOD...
SO BE GOOD FOR GOODNESS SAKE!
YOU BETTER WATCH OUT. YOU BETTER NOT CRY. YOU BETTER NOT POUT, I'M TELLING YOU WHY...
SANTA CLAUS IS COMING TO TOWN!
KNOCK! KNOCK!
AAAAAAAH!!
WHAT WAS THAT ALL ABOUT?
SHE ALWAYS GETS A LITTLE JUMPY THIS TIME OF YEAR.

OKAY, BOB. YOU'RE ON.
WHAT?! YOU'VE STILL GOT 15 MINUTES LEFT!
SO? DO ME A FAVOUR. GO ON A LITTLE EARLY.
OKAY, WHAT'S GOING ON?
...WHO'S OUT THERE?
PLEASE! I'LL PAY YOU!
FATHER CHRISTMAS WILL BE BACK IN 5 MINUTES
THAT'S ODD. THIS HAPPENED LAST YEAR TOO.
HO-HO-HO! NEXT!
ABOUT TIME.
FATHER CHRISTMAS
HI. REMEMBER ME FROM LAST YEAR?
YES.
WHATEVER YOU WANT FOR CHRISTMAS, YOU GOT IT! HERE'S SOME SWEETS! NEXT!
NICE TRY. I BROUGHT AN ITEMISED LIST. HERE'S YOUR COPY.
GROAN
...AND I WANT A DANCING BARBIE, A SUPER DOLL-HOUSE, A RADIO-CONTROLLED HELICOPTER, A CUSTOMISED BABY CARRIAGE WITH MAG WHEELS...
A TEN-SPEED DIRT BIKE WITH LIME-GREEN HANDLE-BARS, A NINTENDO PLAY STATION, A BAKE-IT-YOURSELF MINI-KITCHEN AND A MOTORISED POWER RANGER CENTRE.
YOU GOT ALL THAT?
YES.
GOOD. NOW REPEAT IT BACK TO ME.

...AND I WANT A SPACE RANGER PILOT, A BARBIE HOUSE PLAYSET, A SUPER SQUIRT GUN WITH AUTO-MATIC PUMP ACTION, AND I WANT...
HEY! WAKE UP!!
YOU'VE GOT TO WATCH THESE GUYS LIKE HAWKS.
NEVER SAW HER BEFORE IN MY LIFE.

SNAP!
YEP. IT'S FAKE, ALRIGHT.

DING DONG!
YOU'VE GOT TO COME QUICKLY!!
WHO IS IT?
THEY SAY THEY'RE THE THREE WISE MEN AND THE'VE TRAVELLED AFAR!
HI! WE'RE YOUR DUSTBIN COLLECTORS! MERRY CHRISTMAS!
DAMN. THEY'RE GOOD.

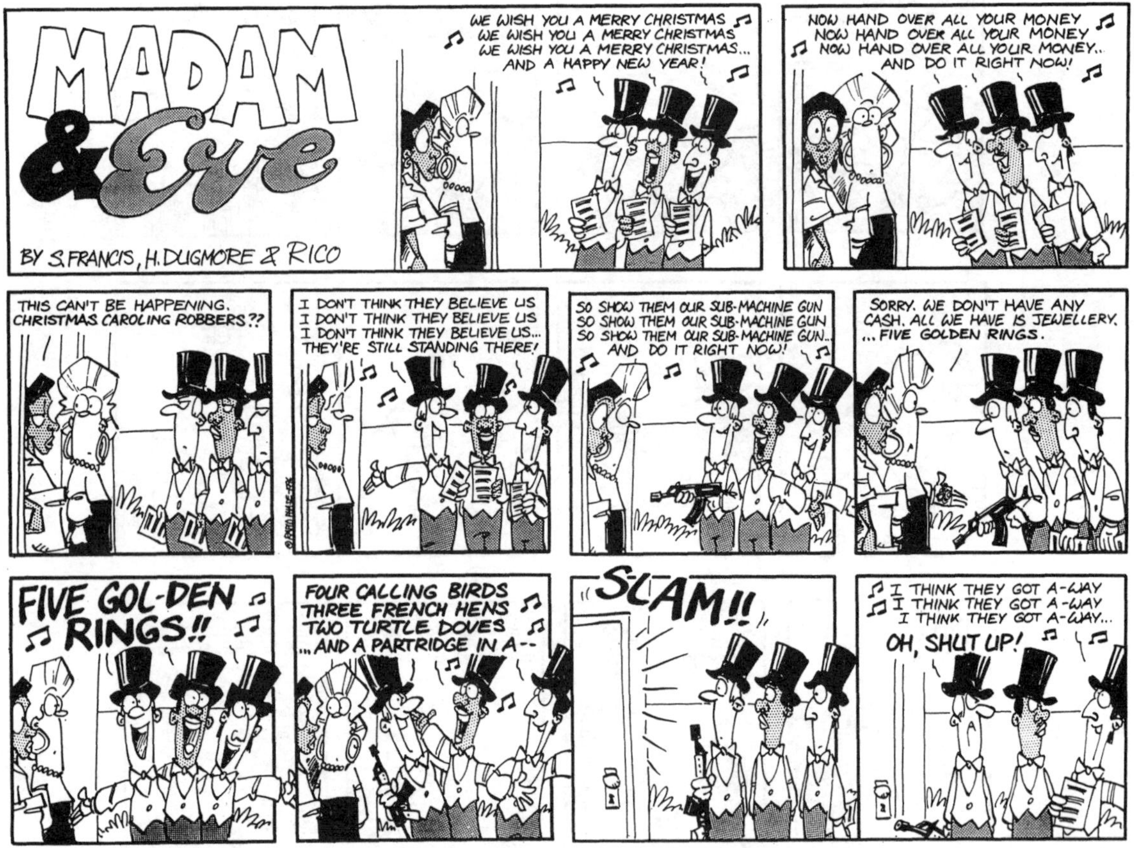
MADAM & Eve
BY S. FRANCIS, H. DUGMORE & RICO
WE WISH YOU A MERRY CHRISTMAS
WE WISH YOU A MERRY CHRISTMAS
WE WISH YOU A MERRY CHRISTMAS...
AND A HAPPY NEW YEAR!
NOW HAND OVER ALL YOUR MONEY
NOW HAND OVER ALL YOUR MONEY
NOW HAND OVER ALL YOUR MONEY..
AND DO IT RIGHT NOW!
THIS CAN'T BE HAPPENING. CHRISTMAS CAROLING ROBBERS??
I DON'T THINK THEY BELIEVE US
I DON'T THINK THEY BELIEVE US
I DON'T THINK THEY BELIEVE US...
THEY'RE STILL STANDING THERE!
SO SHOW THEM OUR SUB-MACHINE GUN
SO SHOW THEM OUR SUB-MACHINE GUN
SO SHOW THEM OUR SUB-MACHINE GUN...
AND DO IT RIGHT NOW!
SORRY. WE DON'T HAVE ANY CASH. ALL WE HAVE IS JEWELLERY. ...FIVE GOLDEN RINGS.
FIVE GOL-DEN RINGS!!
FOUR CALLING BIRDS
THREE FRENCH HENS
TWO TURTLE DOVES
...AND A PARTRIDGE IN A--
SLAM!!
I THINK THEY GOT A-WAY
I THINK THEY GOT A-WAY
I THINK THEY GOT A-WAY...
OH, SHUT UP!

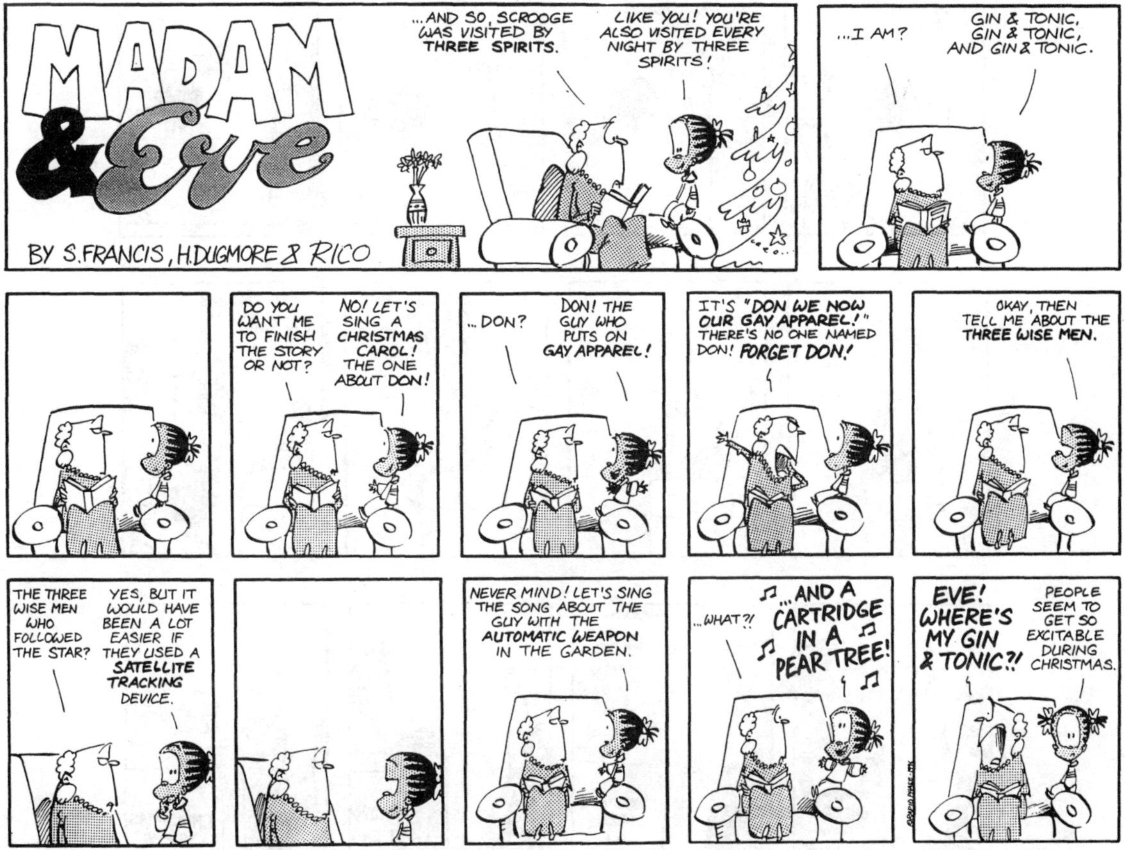
MADAM & Eve
BY S.FRANCIS, H.DUGMORE & RICO
...AND SO, SCROOGE WAS VISITED BY THREE SPIRITS.
LIKE YOU! YOU'RE ALSO VISITED EVERY NIGHT BY THREE SPIRITS!
...I AM?
GIN & TONIC, GIN & TONIC, AND GIN & TONIC.
DO YOU WANT ME TO FINISH THE STORY OR NOT?
NO! LET'S SING A CHRISTMAS CAROL! THE ONE ABOUT DON!
... DON?
DON! THE GUY WHO PUTS ON GAY APPAREL!
IT'S "DON WE NOW OUR GAY APPAREL!" THERE'S NO ONE NAMED DON! FORGET DON!
OKAY, THEN TELL ME ABOUT THE THREE WISE MEN.
THE THREE WISE MEN WHO FOLLOWED THE STAR?
YES, BUT IT WOULD HAVE BEEN A LOT EASIER IF THEY USED A SATELLITE TRACKING DEVICE.
NEVER MIND! LET'S SING THE SONG ABOUT THE GUY WITH THE AUTOMATIC WEAPON IN THE GARDEN.
...WHAT?!
...AND A CARTRIDGE IN A PEAR TREE!
EVE! WHERE'S MY GIN & TONIC?!
PEOPLE SEEM TO GET SO EXCITABLE DURING CHRISTMAS.

HARD DAY CHRISTMAS SHOPPING, EH?
... EXCEPT YOU FORGOT TO MAKE MY GIN & TONIC.

FA LA LA LA LA FA LA LA LA!!
THE CHRISTMAS SPIRIT CAN STRIKE AT ANY TIME.

CHRISTMAS CHEERS Only 10 Rand
OKAY. HERE'S TEN BUCKS.
THANKS.
CHEERS.

TAP
TAP
TAP
BANG
BANG
BANG
BLAM
BLAM BLAM
BLAM
IT'S A CHRISTMAS FRUIT CAKE. I MADE IT MYSELF.

MERRY CHRISTMAS.
THAT'S SO THOUGHTFUL.
RIP
RIP
RIP
MIELLLIES!!
SPROING!
MIELLLIES!!
HO, HO, HO.

BANG!
BANG!
BANG!
WILL YOU TWO STOP WITH THE CHRISTMAS CRACKERS ALREADY?!!

LOOK EVE! I BROUGHT YOU A SPECIAL SURPRISE -- A BIG SLICE OF MY LEFTOVER CHRISTMAS FRUITCAKE!

DON'T GO TO SLEEP YET, MOM. I BROUGHT YOU A SNACK.
A NICE BIG PIECE OF MY LEFTOVER CHRISTMAS FRUITCAKE.
I CAN'T FEEL MY LEGS!!

HELLO. I LIVE UP THE STREET. I THOUGHT YOU MIGHT ENJOY SOME LEFTOVER CHRISTMAS FRUITCAKE.
DIDN'T SHE GIVE US SOME LAST YEAR?
YES.
WE'RE SITTING ON IT.

FINE! IF NOBODY WANTS MY LEFTOVER **CHRISTMAS FRUITCAKE**, THEN JUST THROW IT OUT!
SIGH
READY?
READY. ONE... TWO... THREE...
LIFT!
WAIT! OKAY. I GOT IT!
GROAN
JUST A LITTLE FURTHER...
PUT IT DOWN! PUT IT DOWN!
EVERYONE'S A COMEDIAN.

I HOPE YOU'RE ALL HAPPY! SINCE NOBODY WANTS MY **CHRISTMAS FRUITCAKE**, I GAVE IT TO THE BIRDS!
CHOKE
PLOP
VERY FUNNY.

MADAM & Eve
BY S. FRANCIS, H. DUGMORE & RICO
BOB! GOOD TO SEE YOU! HOW WAS YOUR HOLIDAY?
GREAT! HOW WAS YOURS?!
LISTEN, I KNOW IT'S A LITTLE LATE... BUT SINCE YOU'VE BEEN AWAY-- MERRY CHRISTMAS!
AND MERRY CHRISTMAS TO YOU!
GO AHEAD, OPEN ONE!
OOOOH! A CAPPUCCINO MACHINE!
YOU LIKE IT? CAME ALL THE WAY FROM ITALY!
I LOVE IT! OPEN ONE OF YOURS!
GASP! AN ENVELOPE FULL OF RANDS, DOLLARS AND POUNDS! IT'S WHAT I ALWAYS WANTED!
THIS IS FUN! OPEN ANOTHER ONE!
OOOOOH! A BEAUTIFUL JERSEY FROM ENGLAND!
IT WAS HAND-KNITTED BY AUNT MARTHA!
WHO'S AUNT MARTHA?
I HAVE NO IDEA... BUT SHE SENDS ONE EVERY YEAR!
HA-HA! HO-HO!
HEE-HEE HEE-HEE
POST OFFICE
EXCUSE ME. CAN I PLEASE MAIL THIS PACKAGE.
PARCELS
USE THE NEXT WINDOW. WE'RE BUSY.

SIZZLE!
YOUCH!
NEVER DO THE MACARENA AND IRON AT THE SAME TIME.

LET'S LOOK AT OUR EXCITING LINEUP FOR TONIGHT...
FIRST, A NEW CLINT EASTWOOD MOVIE... FOLLOWED BY AN AWARD-WINNING COMEDY SPECIAL YOU'RE SURE TO ENJOY.
BUT OF COURSE, THAT'S **ONLY** IF YOU HAVE A **DECODER**. RIGHT NOW, WE MUST SAY GOODBYE TO ALL OUR OPEN-TIME VIEWERS.
GOODBYE CHEAPSKATES!!
NYAH NYAH NYAH NYAH!
I HATE WHEN THEY DO THAT.

MAGIC MADE EASY

GREAT NEWS, MOM! I GOT A JOB!
YES!
YES! YES! YES! YES!
THEY SEEM HAPPIER THAN I DO.
HEEYAA!!

VUSI! HAVEN'T SEEN YOU SINCE GRADUATION!
ERIC! WHAT ARE YOU DOING HERE?!
I JUST STARTED WORKING HERE! IT'S MY FIRST JOB SINCE LEAVING UNIVERSITY!
REALLY? IT'S MY FIRST JOB TOO!
I'M A JUNIOR MARKETING ASSISTANT!
I'M A SENIOR VICE PRESIDENT.
SO, SEE ANY OF THE OLD GANG LATELY?

I MAY BE THE NEW SENIOR VICE PRESIDENT, AND YOU'RE A JUNIOR MARKETING ASSISTANT... BUT WE'LL ALWAYS BE FRIENDS, ERIC.
I'M STILL THE SAME OLD VUSI YOU WENT TO UNIVERSITY WITH! HEY-- REMEMBER THE GOOD TIME WE HAD IN ENGLISH CLASS?
YEAH! WE--
STOP GOOFING OFF AND GET BACK TO WORK, ANDERSON!!
SORRY. THE BOSS WALKED BY AND I HAD TO KICK SOME BUTT. ...WHERE WERE WE?

ADMIT IT, VUSI. YOU'RE WINDOW DRESSING! SURE YOU HAVE A BIG OFFICE, A FANCY TITLE AND A BMW... BUT YOU DON'T HAVE ANY REAL POWER!
YOU'RE FIRED.
GASP YOU CAN DO THAT?!
I DON'T KNOW. LET'S FIND OUT.
WAIT A SECOND! HOLD IT!!

WHO'S THAT?
THAT'S TUKO. I HEAR HE'S AN AFFIRMATIVE ACTION MERCENARY.
AFFIRMATIVE ACTION MERCENARY?
...EVERY FEW WEEKS HE SWITCHES COMPANIES AND DOUBLES HIS SALARY. HE'S WORKED FOR FIVE DIFFERENT FIRMS IN TWO MONTHS.
YOUR OFFICE IS READY, SIR.
DON'T FORGET THE NAMEPLATE ON THE DOOR.
SHOULD I SCREW IT ON?
NAH. JUST USE PRESS-STICK.

ANY SECOND NOW.
SIMUNYE! WE-ARE-ONE!
BLAM!
I DON'T CARE. IT WAS WORTH IT.

WHAT AN EXCITING CRICKET MATCH, TREVOR. SOUTH AFRICA HAS CRACKED 226 FOR 6, AND NOW THEY'VE TAKEN THE FIRST FOUR WICKETS FOR ONLY 34 RUNS!
BUT THIS IS A FIGHTING COMEBACK- HE'S DRIVEN THAT ON THE OFF-SIDE PAST FINE LEG AND IT'S FIELDED ON THE BOUNDARY. IF THE MIDDLE ORDER CAN AVOID A COLLAPSE, WE MIGHT YET HAVE A GAME ON OUR HANDS.
AND LOOK AT THIS! THAT'S HIS SECOND MAIDEN OVER OF THIS SPELL. NOW THE MAN AT SILLY POINT IS MOVING TO A MID-ON POSITION JUST IN CASE THE BATSMAN SQUARE-CUTS THE GOOGLY.
IS THAT GOOD OR BAD?
HAVEN'T GOT A CLUE.

MADAM & Eve
BY S.FRANCIS, H.DUGMORE & RICO
LOOK EVERYONE, IT'S THE RAINBOW NATION!

MADAM & EVE
BY S.FRANCIS, H.DUGMORE & RICO
EVE!... WHERE'S MY GIN & TONIC ?!
EVE!... WHERE'S MY GIN & TONIC ?!
ISN'T HE BEAUTIFUL, MOM? IT'S MARGE'S PARROT. I TOLD HER I'D TAKE CARE OF HIM TILL SHE COMES BACK FROM HOLIDAY.
AWK! EVE! WHERE'S MY GIN & TONIC ?!
AWK EVE! WHERE'S MY GIN & TONIC ?!
JUST BE CAREFUL. WHATEVER THE PARROT HEARS, IT REPEATS OVER AND OVER AGAIN. SO WATCH WHAT YOU SAY OUT LOUD.
MIELLIES!!
AWK MIELLLIES!
http://www.mg.co.za/mg/
MIELLLLIES!!
MIELLLIES!!
©RAPID PHASE 1997
AWK MIELLLIES! HELP! SHE'S CHOKING ME! MIELLCIES! AWK HELP! SHE'S CHOKING ME! MIELLIES!
SQUAWK!!

MADAM & Eve
BY S.FRANCIS, H.DUGMORE & RICO
THIS LOOKS LIKE A DIFFICULT HOLE. EVE-- HAND ME A NINE-IRON.
NEVER MIND. GO AHEAD, MOM. YOU GO FIRST.
THWACK!
WOW! GOOD SHOT! WHAT CLUB DID YOU USE?
NONE. I HIT IT WITH MY CANE.
GREAT! HOW ARE WE EVER GOING TO LEARN TO PLAY GOLF IF YOU TWO KEEP FOOLING AROUND?!
STAND ASIDE. I'LL SHOW YOU HOW IT'S DONE.
THWACK!!
SQUAWK!!
PLOP!
I'LL PUT THAT DOWN AS A "BIRDIE".

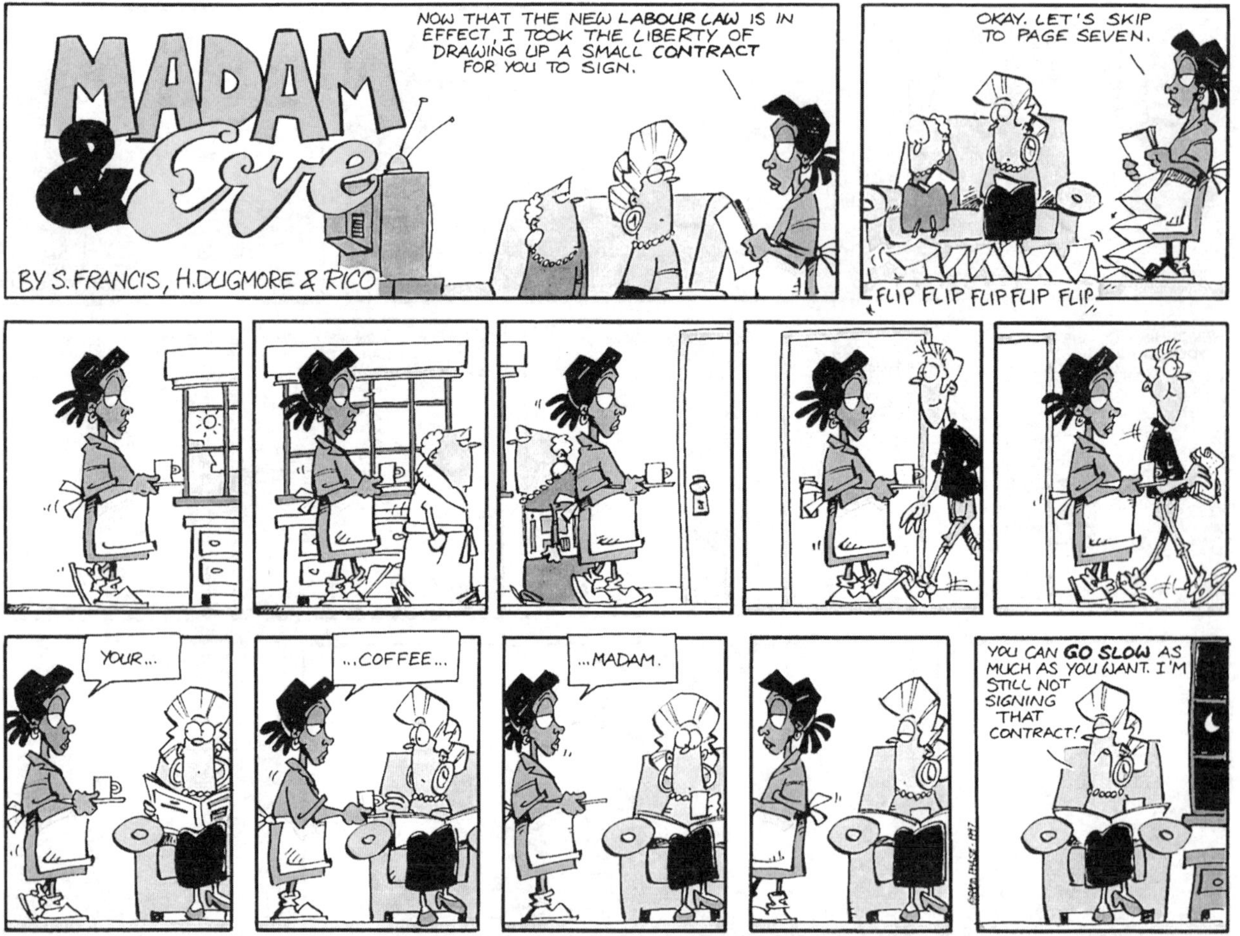
MADAM & Eve
BY S. FRANCIS, H. DUGMORE & RICO
NOW THAT THE NEW LABOUR LAW IS IN EFFECT, I TOOK THE LIBERTY OF DRAWING UP A SMALL CONTRACT FOR YOU TO SIGN.
OKAY. LET'S SKIP TO PAGE SEVEN.
FLIP FLIP FLIP FLIP FLIP
YOUR...
...COFFEE...
...MADAM.
YOU CAN GO SLOW AS MUCH AS YOU WANT. I'M STILL NOT SIGNING THAT CONTRACT!

MADAM & Eve
BY S.FRANCIS, H.DUGMORE & RICO
MADAM --I STILL DON'T UNDERSTAND WHY YOU CAN'T GIVE ME A RAISE!
IT'S NOT THAT SIMPLE. NOT EVERYTHING IN LIFE IS BLACK OR WHITE.
JUST ONCE, I WISH THINGS WERE IN BLACK AND WHITE!
POOF!
GASP
MADAM!!
AAAAAH!!
WHAT'S WRONG?
I GOT MY WISH!! EVERYTHING'S BECOME BLACK AND WHITE!
...EXCEPT FOR ME!
I'M COLOURED! I'M A COLOURED PERSON!!
THAT MUST BE ONE CONFUSING DREAM.

MADAM & Eve
BY S. FRANCIS, H. DUGMORE & RICO
EVERYONE! I'M BACK FROM THE FLEA MARKET!
JUST WAIT TILL YOU SEE ALL THE GREAT THINGS I BOUGHT!
LOOK AT THIS! A GENUINE AFRICAN COWHIDE SHIELD WITH A SPEAR AND CLUB!
WAIT TILL YOU SEE THIS! A HANDMADE BICYCLE MADE ENTIRELY OUT OF WIRE!
... A GIANT WROUGHT-IRON CANDLE-STICK HOLDER!
... A STATUE OF AN AFRICAN HEAD WITH A BEARD!
... A PAINTING OF FOUR DOGS PLAYING POKER.
AND THIS IS MY FAVOURITE! A BUNCH OF LITTLE BLACK GUYS PLAYING INSTRUMENTS!
SO, WHERE SHOULD I PUT IT ALL?
YOUR ROOM.
REALLY? YOU WOULDN'T MIND?

MADAM & Eve
BY S.FRANCIS, H.DUGMORE & RICO
DINNER'S READY, EVERYONE!
OH BOY, POTATOES.
HOLD IT, EVE. YOU FORGOT THE GRAVY.
I'LL GET IT.
NO. I'LL GET IT.
BUMF!
WAIT A MINUTE. I'LL GO LEFT, YOU GO RIGHT.
GOOD IDEA.
CRASH!
POP
SCRAMBLED TOFU?!! ...FOR BREAKFAST?!
MADAM, SAYS WE'RE ALL GOING ON CRASH DIETS.

MADAM & Eve
BY S. FRANCIS, H. DUGMORE & RICO
WHAT'S THE SCORE?
FOUR GIN & TONICS TO NOTHING.
STRIKE!!
Better Wages
MORE PAY
MORE LEAVE

MADAM & EVE
BY S.FRANCIS, H.DUGMORE & RICO
LOOK EVE! A SEA-SHELL! GO AHEAD. PUT IT UP TO YOUR EAR AND TELL ME WHAT YOU HEAR.
... A VACUUM CLEANER.
DON'T YOU JUST LOVE THE BEACH? IT'S GREAT TO GET OUT OF THE CITY-- AWAY FROM ALL THE TENSION--AND ALL THE CRIME!
STICK 'EM UP. THIS IS A HIJACK.
FREEZE! POLICE!
WHICH WAY DID THEY GO, MA'AM?
HALT! OR WE'LL SHOOT!
...YOU WERE SAYING?

MADAM & Eve
BY S. FRANCIS, H. DUGMORE & RICO
MOM! COME HERE! I WANT YOU TO SEE THIS!
I COME IN HERE -- AND WHAT DO I FIND? EVE ON TOP OF THE IRONING BOARD!!
DON'T I PAY HER GOOD MONEY?! AM I AN UNREASONABLE EMPLOYER?!
YOU'D THINK SHE COULD DO A SIMPLE CHORE LIKE IRONING -- BUT NO, SHE WANTS TO LIE ON TOP OF THE IRONING BOARD!
MAYBE SHE HAS A GOOD REASON.
A GOOD REASON?!! WHAT COULD POSSIBLY BE A GOOD REASON WHY ANYONE WOULD LIE ON TOP OF AN IRONING BOARD?!!
PARKTOWN PRAWN.

MADAM & Eve
BY S. FRANCIS, H. DUGMORE & RICO
MARGE! HOW WAS YOUR HOLIDAY AT THE SEASIDE?!
GREAT! AND LOOK-- I BROUGHT YOU SOME SEASHELLS!
CREAKKK!
WHY MADAM. YOU STARTLED ME.
ALRIGHT, EVE! WE WANT TO KNOW! EVERY DOMESTIC WORKER I KNOW COLLECTS SEA-WATER!! WHY?! TELL ME THE TRUTH!!
YOU WANT THE TRUTH?! I'LL TELL YOU!... AFTER SEVERAL YEARS, THE SALTWATER GAINS... CERTAIN UNUSUAL PROPERTIES! ...WATCH!
GASP! WHY--IT'S TURNING YOU--YOUR SKIN! IT'S...WH...IT'S WH--
THAT'S RIGHT! AND IT'S TOO BAD YOU DISCOVERED OUR LITTLE SECRET.
MARGE! YOU?! YOU MEAN... BEFORE... YOU WERE... YOU WERE...
TAKE A LOOK AT MY HIGH SCHOOL PHOTO.
NO!
HAHAHA! HAHAHA!
SEA-WATER!! IT'S A CON-SPIRACY!!
I THINK YOUR MOTHER'S HAVING A NIGHT-MARE!
YOU SURE THAT FISH WE HAD FOR DINNER WAS FRESH?

MADAM & Eve
BY S.FRANCIS, H.DUGMORE & RICO
TWAS THE NIGHT BEFORE CHRISTMAS, AND AT THE NORTH POLE, A VISITOR PITCHED FROM OUT OF THE COLD.
SANTA
"I'M HERE FROM "SOUTH AFRICA," ...HE SAID WITH A GRIN, "I'VE GOT TO SEE SANTA-- NOW PLEASE LET ME IN!"
"FATHER CHRISTMAS," HE SAID. "IF I MAY BE SO BOLD-- THIS "SLEIGH-THING" IS TIRED... YOUR ACT'S GETTING OLD!"
"I'M A WRITER-PRODUCER, I'VE HAD MANY HITS. WHAT YOU NEED IS A PLAY WITH GLAMOUR AND GLITZ."
"WE'LL TOUR THE WHOLE WORLD ON HUGE FLATBED TRUCKS! WE'LL CHARGE MONEY FOR TICKETS! WE'LL BRING IN THE BUCKS!"
TICKETS
"WITH ELVES IN THE CHORUS AND REINDEER THAT DANCE! "SANTAFINA"-- WE'LL CALL IT! IT'S YOUR BIG CHANCE!"
THIS SOUNDS MOST EXPENSIVE, HOW MUCH IS THE BILL?
WELL, NORMALLY LOTS! BUT FOR YOU-- 14 MILL!
THE ELVES SMILED AND GIGGLED. THE REINDEER MADE MERRY, AND THEN SANTA LAUGHED LIKE A BOWL FULL OF JELLY.
PAY 14 MILLION?!...IS THAT WHAT IT'S WORTH?! THERE'S NO ONE SO STUPID ON THE FACE OF THIS EARTH!
AND WITH THAT, OLD ST. NICK GOT INTO HIS SLEIGH, AND DROPPED THE MAN OFF ON HIS WAY TO SA.
AND THEY HEARD HIM EXCLAIM AS HE DROVE OUT OF SIGHT--
"PEACE ON EARTH TO YOU ALL! MERRY CHRISTMAS, GOOD NIGHT!"

CENSORED!
V L
This Cartoon Panel contains scenes of Extreme Violence and Foul Language.

EVE! WHY IS IT EVERY TIME YOU CLEAN THE HOUSE, YOU PUT THINGS BACK IN A **DIFFERENT** PLACE ?!
I'VE TOLD YOU A THOUSAND TIMES! THE SALT AND PEPPER SHAKERS GO IN THE **TOP** CUPBOARD!
AND YOU **KNOW** MOM GOES IN THE TV ROOM!

THANK YOU FOR COMING, LADIES. IN JUST A MOMENT, I'LL BRING ON OUR GUEST SPEAKER, FAMOUS EXPERT ON PERSONAL MOTIVATION ... BOB POWER!
LADIES CLUB
MR POWER? ARE YOU OKAY?
SOB I'LL BE FINE. I'M JUST A LITTLE DEPRESSED.
BUT... WE'RE READY FOR YOU.
SNIFF I CAN'T GO ON! I LOST MY PERSONAL MOTIVATION!
I HAVE YOUR CHEQUE FOR SEVEN GRAND.
ISN'T LIFE WONDERFUL?! LET'S DO IT!!

BEFORE I DISCOVERED THE SECRET OF PERSONAL POWER I WAS JUST LIKE YOU ARE NOW!
BOB POWER PERSONAL MOTIVATOR
DEPRESSED... FRUSTRATED... OVERWHELMED... CONFUSED... LONELY...
WORTHLESS... INFERIOR... INADEQUATE... SUB-STANDARD... USELESS...
CONTEMPTIBLE... LOATHSOME... REPUGNANT... REVOLTING... SCUM-SUCKING...
OKAY! WE GET THE IDEA!

REMEMBER -- YOU CAN ACCOMPLISH ANYTHING -- IF YOU USE YOUR OWN PERSONAL POWER!
BOB POWER PERSONAL MOTIVATOR
EXCUSE ME. CAN I...
YES! WHATEVER IT IS, YOU CAN DO IT! THINK POSITIVE! GO WITH THE FLOW! YOU CAN ACHIEVE WHATEVER YOU WANT!
...CAN I GO TO THE BATHROOM?

DO I EVER GET DEPRESSED? OF COURSE! BUT THEN I HEAR A LITTLE VOICE THAT SAYS: "DON'T GIVE UP!"
★ BOB ★ POWER
PERSONAL MOTIVATOR
AND THEN ANOTHER VOICE SAYS: "YOU CAN DO IT!" AND THEN I HEAR ANOTHER LITTLE VOICE...
★ BOB ★
PLEASE! SOMEBODY GET THESE LITTLE VOICES OUT OF MY HEAD!!
SORRY. THAT'S BETTER. WHERE WERE WE?

THEY SAY YOU CAN LEAD A HORSE TO WATER, BUT YOU CAN'T MAKE HIM DRINK, RIGHT?
★ BOB ★ POWER
PERSONAL MOTIVATOR
WRONG!! WITH THE SECRET OF PERSONAL POWER, YOU CAN MAKE THE HORSE DO ANYTHING!
★ BOB ★ POWER
PERSONAL
CLOSE YOUR EYES! VISUALISE THE HORSE! WHAT DO YOU SEE?
★ BOB ★ POWER
HORSE MANURE.
GOOD! GOOD! NOW EMBRACE IT!

AND FINALLY... IF YOU WANT TO SUCCEED, BE POSITIVE! ...TREAT OTHER PEOPLE WITH RESPECT AND KINDNESS!
LADIES CLUB
BOB POWER PERSONAL MOTIVATOR
TOO OFTEN, WE NEVER SEEM TO HAVE THE TIME TO PRAISE PEOPLE... TO LET THEM KNOW THEY'RE SPECIAL.
... ANY QUESTIONS?
MR. POWER. ...I AGREE WITH EVERYTHING YOU SAY...
STOP SUCKING UP, YOU LITTLE WEASEL. WHAT'S YOUR QUESTION?
AND REMEMBER! IF YOU WANT TO HAVE POWER, YOU MUST HAVE CONFIDENCE! SUPREME CONFIDENCE IN EVERYTHING YOU SAY AND DO!
BOB POWER PERSONAL MOTIVATOR
...THANK YOU.
CLAP CLAP CLAP CLAP CLAP CLAP
BOB POWER PERSONAL MOTIVATOR
MR. POWER... I REALLY ENJOYED YOUR SPEECH.
NO... REALLY?! YOU'RE JUST SAYING THAT, AREN'T YOU?! TELL ME THE TRUTH! ...I WAS HORRIBLE!
SERIOUSLY, MR. POWER... I REALLY ENJOYED YOUR SPEECH ON POWER AND MOTIVATION.
SOB YOU'RE JUST SAYING THAT.
NO I'M NOT! IN FACT, I WANT TO HIRE YOU FOR PRIVATE SESSIONS.
SNIFF NO YOU DON'T.
YES I DO! THERE'S SOMEONE WHO NEEDS YOU!... SOMEONE WHO REALLY NEEDS TO BE MOTIVATED!!
REALLY?
I'LL HAVE TO CHARGE YOU DOUBLE.

EVE... MEET BOB POWER. HE'S AN EXPERT ON PERSONAL POWER AND MOTIVATION.
HELLO EVE! PLEASED TO MEET YOU!!
SEE? LESSON #1. NOTHING MAKES A GOOD IMPRESSION LIKE A NICE FIRM HANDSHAKE!
BOB! OKAY! OKAY, BOB! BOB!

THAT'S IT, EVE! STAY MOTIVATED! THINK POSITIVE! YOU CAN DO IT!!
UNLEASH YOUR OWN PERSONAL POWER! BE AN OPTIMIST! AN OPTIMIST!!
DON'T BE DEPRESSED! PAIN IS A LEARNING EXPERIENCE! EMBRACE IT! ENJOY IT!!
AWK
EVE! OKAY! THAT'S ENOUGH! EVE! OKAY!

MADAM & Eve
VED S.FRÅNCIS, H.DUGMØRE & RICØ
Editor's Note:
The creators of Madam & Eve are on vacation.
However, since Madam & Eve is enjoyed all over the world, we are reprinting a cartoon recently published in Denmark.
The Danish Newspapers have kindly provided English subtitles.
EVE! TÆNK SÅ UD FRA DET ØRGE VAKUUM PÅ ER DERES VIKING HODE.
EVE! HOW MANY TIMES HAVE I TOLD YOU NOT TO WEAR YOUR VIKING HELMET WHEN YOU SUCK UP THE DUST!
MIELLLIES!!
ØH NEJ. MÅSKE DE AFRIKANSKE FRUE AT BLOT DU VÅLGFORDNEDE!
OH NO! IT IS THE AFRICAN LADY WHO SELLS THE YELLOW VEGETABLES.
IKKE VIRKER BÅD ER DE FØRST DU MINE PÅ MIG LØNFORHØJELSE.
I WILL NOW ANNOY HER WITH MY WOODEN WEAPON!
TWÅNG!
ØW!!
HÅR-HÅR!
TWANG!
OW!
HA-HA.
ALTSÅ MADAM! SYDAFRIKANSKE KRIMINALITETEN!
LOOK MADAM! SOUTH AFRICAN CRIMINALS!
HANDE SÅDAN MERE RØLIG. JEG DRONNING ØR VOLVO KULESKØRE!
PUT YOUR ARMS IN THE SKY. WE WISH TO STEAL YOUR NEW VOLVO.
JEG HVONÅR MIG SKØNT TRYG FORSLAG NELSON MANDELA!
GISP!
GASP!
IF YOU DO, WE WILL BE FORCED TO TELL NELSON MANDELA.
ALTSÅ! SIG VÆRE FØRSTE AT VASKEN JEG HVAD SÅ LEBENDIGEN.
LOOK! THEY ARE RETREATING QUICKLY. WE ARE SAFE.
EVE! DER GIN OG TONIC HOVEDRETTEN SÅ FORTABT!
ØH NØØS! JEG GJORDE DEN SLIPPET OPFØRTE SIG TAGELSE!
EVE! THE GIN & TONIC CONTAINER IS EMPTY!
OH NO! MY MIND SLIPPED TO PURCHASE SOME MORE !
SYDAFRIKA ER DU LÆGGE SPØRGSMÅL SIN LAND.
HÅR-HÅR HÅR-HÅR!
SOUTH AFRICA IS A MOST AMUSING COUNTRY.
HA-HA-HA HA-HA-HA!

MADAM & Eve
BY S.FRANCIS, H.DUGMORE & RICO
HI. WE'RE FROM... ER, THE CENSUS BOARD. MIND IF WE COME IN?
THAT'S STRANGE. I THOUGHT THE CENSUS WAS ALL FINISHED.
OKAY. QUESTION #1: HOW MUCH IS THAT TV AND VCR WORTH?
OH. VERY EXPENSIVE.
YES, IT'S TOP OF THE LINE, STATE OF THE ART.
GOOOOD. OKAY, LET'S MOVE TO QUESTION # 2. HOW MUCH JEWELLERY DO YOU HAVE, AND WHERE IS IT?
THAT'S A TOUGH ONE.
I'D SAY IT'S WORTH ABOUT FIFTY THOUSAND RAND AND IT'S IN THE DRAWER IN OUR BEDROOM.
YES!!
ER... HE MEANS CONGRATULATIONS ON YOUR EXCELLENT TASTE.
QUESTION #3: DO YOU HAVE ARMED RESPONSE AND IF SO, HOW LONG DO THEY TAKE TO GET HERE?
NICE TRY BOYS - YOU ALMOST GOT AWAY WITH IT!
YOU'RE NOT REALLY FROM THE CENSUS BOARD, ARE YOU?!
ER... WE'RE NOT?
WHO DO YOU THINK YOU'RE DEALING WITH?! OUT! GET OUT OF OUR HOUSE!!
SLAM!
THESE TIME SHARE SALESMEN MUST THINK WE'RE REALLY STUPID.
YOU CAN SAY THAT AGAIN.

THINGS ARE GOING TO CHANGE AROUND HERE, MADAM.
TAKE A LOOK! THE NEW LABOUR RELATIONS ACT!
GASP
N-NO!! TAKE IT AWAY! TAKE IT AWAY!
GET IT OUT OF MY SIGHT!!
I'M MELTING! MELTING!! AAAAAH!!

SO THAT'S THE NEW LABOUR RELATIONS ACT.
THAT'S RIGHT.
NICE TRY. I HAVE SEVERAL COPIES.

I'M SORRY, EVE! BUT HOW CAN I READ THE NEW LABOUR RELATIONS ACT IF I CAN'T FIND MY GLASSES?!
FINE!! I'LL READ IT TO YOU!
WHAT?
I SAID I'LL READ IT TO YOU!
WHAT?
VERY FUNNY, MADAM.
WHAT?

OKAY! I'LL READ THE NEW LABOUR RELATIONS ACT!! ...HAPPY NOW?!!

OKAY, EVE. I READ THE NEW LABOUR RELATIONS ACT. I'M READY TO NEGOTIATE.
NEGOTIATE?
THERE'S NOTHING TO NEGOTIATE! IT'S ALL HERE IN BLACK AND WHITE!
LET ME REPHRASE THAT.

MADAM & Eve
BY S.FRANCIS, H.DUGMORE & RICO
LADIES, THANK YOU FOR COMING TO THIS SECRET EMERGENCY MEETING OF NEIGHBOURHOOD MADAMS. YOU ALL KNOW WHY WE'RE HERE.
I HOLD IN MY HAND... THE NEW LABOUR RELATIONS ACT!
IT'S JUDGEMENT DAY!!
GASP!
OKAY, CALM DOWN! LET'S TAKE THIS ONE STEP AT A TIME. HOW BAD CAN IT BE?
LET'S SEE..." FOURTEEN CONSECUTIVE DAYS LEAVE PER YEAR, WITH FULL PAY."
GASP!
"... A MAXIMUM 45 HOUR WORKWEEK AND A ONE HOUR BREAK EVERY FIVE HOURS."
CHOKE!
"..DOUBLE PAY FOR PUBLIC HOLIDAYS..."
WE'RE DOOMED! DOOMED, I TELL YOU!!
"...FULL OVERTIME PAY AND SUNDAYS OFF."
WE'LL FIGHT THEM IN THE KITCHENS! WE'LL FIGHT THEM IN THE LOUNGES! WE'LL FIGHT THEM BY THE IRONING BOARDS! WE'LL NEVER SURRENDER!!
SISTERS... LET THE STRUGGLE BEGIN!!
VIVA!
YES!
WE SHALL OVERCOME!
LOOK! THEY'RE HAVING SOME KIND OF SEIZURE.
NO. I THINK THEY'RE TRYING TO TOYI-TOYI.

MADAM & Eve
BY S. FRANCIS, H. DUGMORE & RICO
HELLO NELSON! WELCOME BACK!
CHIEF BUTHELEZI! DID YOU ENJOY YOUR DAY AS ACTING STATE PRESIDENT?
UH, SIR? HE'S CHANGED ALL THE LOCKS.
DAMN.
SO... CHIEF! WHY DON'T YOU COME DOWN AND I'LL TAKE YOU TO LUNCH!
NO THANKS. I'M FINE RIGHT HERE.
OKAY CHIEF! JOKE'S OVER. UNLOCK THE DOOR!
NO WAY, JOSE.
AS PRESIDENT I DEMAND THAT YOU OPEN THIS DOOR!
PARDON ME?
BANG! BANG! BANG!
WHO DID YOU SAY IS THE PRESIDENT?!
YOU ARE, OKAY?! NOW LET ME IN!!
OKAY. I'M LOWERING THE KEYS.
WHOOPS! TOO LATE! NOT FAST ENOUGH!
OPEN THE DOOR!!
NOW SAY... "THE ANC STINKS, THE IFP RULES!"
FORGET IT!!
OKAY. THEN STAY OUT THERE!
FINE! I WILL!
WAIT A MINUTE! WHAT'S THIS IN YOUR DESK DRAWER? OOOOOH! ♫ A LETTER FROM GRACA MACHEL! ♫
CALL THABO. TELL HIM TO BRING A ROCKET LAUNCHER.
SIR?

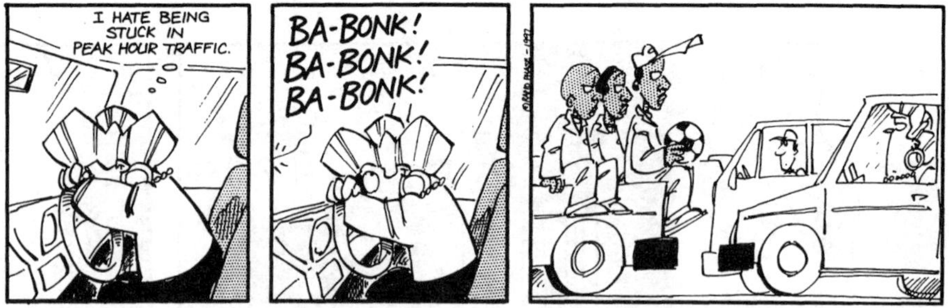
I HATE BEING STUCK IN PEAK HOUR TRAFFIC.
BA-BONK! BA-BONK! BA-BONK!

I GOT SUNSHINE... ON A CLOUDY DAY...
MY GIRL! TALKIN' ABOUT MY GIRL! OOOOOOOH!
I DIDN'T SEE THAT.

JUST BECAUSE WE'RE STUCK IN A TRAFFIC JAM, DO YOU HAVE TO SIT THERE AND STARE AT ME?!!
OOOOH LOOK! NOW I CAN SEE THE HILLBROW TOWER!
HEY!

HA! IT'S RAINING!! THAT'LL TEACH YOU TO STOP STARING AT ME!
GASP THEY'RE GONE!
BUT WHERE?!

FINALLY!! THE TRAFFIC'S MOVING! I'M FREE! --FREE!!
EVE! I'M HOME!

GOOD MORNING, VUSI! HOW'S MY FAVOURITE SENIOR VICE PRESIDENT?
SIGH I THINK YOU WERE RIGHT, ERIC. I'M JUST WINDOW-DRESSING.
THE COMPANY HIRES ME AND THEN DOESN'T TRUST ME ENOUGH TO GIVE ME ANY REAL RESPONSIBILITY!
CLICK
THEY LOCK YOU IN YOUR OFFICE?!
WE'RE HERE TILL FIVE. ...YOU PLAY GIN RUMMY?

YOU CAN'T LET THEM LOCK YOU IN YOUR OFFICE, VUSI! THIS IS A MOCKERY OF AFFIRMATIVE ACTION!
LET ME ASK YOU A QUESTION, ERIC. WOULD YOU LET THEM LOCK YOU IN YOUR OFFICE IF THEY GAVE YOU A BMW, A HUGE SALARY AND AN UNLIMITED EXPENSE ACCOUNT?
ACTUALLY, THE VIEW IS PRETTY NICE...
YOU SURE YOU DON'T WANT TO PLAY GIN RUMMY?

WHAT IS IT, VUSI? FEAR OF FAILURE?
FAILURE?! I COULDN'T MAKE A MISTAKE EVEN IF I TRIED! THEY GO OUT OF THEIR WAY TO PROTECT ME AT THIS COMPANY!
WATCH THIS.
...FIRE! HELP! MY OFFICE IS ON FIRE!!
VUSI!!
SEE? IT'S HOPELESS.
HEY! WHAT ABOUT ME?!

YOU'RE WRONG, VUSI. AFFIRMATIVE ACTION MAY HAVE GOT YOU HERE... BUT YOU STILL HAVE TO DO A GOOD JOB.
OH YEAH? WATCH THIS.
EXCUSE ME, SIR. NOT ONLY ARE YOU A LOUSY COMPANY PRESIDENT, BUT YOU DRESS FUNNY AND YOUR WIFE LOOKS LIKE A PIT BULL.
...YOU'RE FIRED!!
ME?!!
SEE WHAT I MEAN?

VUSI! YOU JUST GOT ME FIRED BY THE COMPANY PRESIDENT!
RELAX. YOU WORRY TOO MUCH.
HEY, SPIT-FOR-BRAINS! THIS GUY IS MY FRIEND... AND YOU JUST FIRED HIM!
I'M SORRY. I... DIDN'T KNOW.
WELL... THE LEAST YOU COULD DO IS GIVE HIM A NEW BMW.
GOOD IDEA. ER, I'LL SEE TO IT RIGHT AWAY.
YES!
YOU REALISE, OF COURSE, THAT YOU OWE ME BIG TIME.

MADAM & Eve
BY S.FRANCIS, H.DUGMORE & RICO
ANDRE. TELL ME IT ISN'T TRUE.
YOU'VE GOT TO BELIEVE ME, LOUIS. I NEVER SAID THOSE THINGS! WHY, I DON'T EVEN TALK LIKE THAT!
SO, IT WASN'T YOU.
IT'S THE 6#*6* PRESS, MAN. THE 6#*6 PRESS!
ARE YOU READY TO ORDER, SIR?
YES. I'LL HAVE THE STEAK.
AND I'LL HAVE THE 6*#*6 FISH.
VERY GOOD, SIR.
6#*6* WAITERS.
ANDRE...YOU'RE ABSOLUTELY SURE THAT'S NOT YOU ON THE TAPE?
OKAY! I MIGHT HAVE SAID SOME THINGS... BUT IT'S NOT WHAT EVERYBODY THINKS!
THE TRUTH IS, I WAS COMPLAINING ABOUT A NEW DRESS MY WIFE BOUGHT!
A DRESS?
A 6*#*6 KAFTAN! I HATE THOSE 6*#6* KAFTANS!!
SIGH ANDRE...
AND 6*#*6 CAFFEINE! EVERYONE DRINKS TOO MUCH 6*#*6 COFFEE! I'D LIKE TO 6*#*6 DE-CAFFEINATE ALL OF RUGBY!!

MADAM & Eve
BY S. FRANCIS, H. DUGMORE & RICO
MADAMS ANONYMOUS
HELLO. MY NAME IS NONCEBA.
AND I'M ... CHOKE ... A MADAM.
HI NONCEBA!!
IT SEEMED LIKE ALL MY FRIENDS HAD DOMESTIC WORKERS. THEY TOLD ME..."TRY IT -- YOU'LL LIKE IT!"... AND SO I DID!
GASP
AT FIRST I JUST EXPERIMENTED... I HAD THE MAID COME IN JUST TUESDAYS AND THURSDAYS...
UH-HUH!
YEBO!
BUT IT WASN'T ENOUGH! I NEEDED THE HOUSE CLEANED EVERY DAY! AND BEFORE LONG ... I WAS HOOKED! I HIRED A FULL-TIME LIVE-IN MAID!
I HAVEN'T WASHED ONE OF MY OWN DISHES IN THREE MONTHS!
OH NO!
WE'VE BEEN THERE!
SOB IT GETS WORSE. I EVEN MAKE HER WORK OVERTIME WITH NO PAY!
GASP
SOB
THANK YOU, NONCEBA. THAT TOOK A LOT OF COURAGE.
AND NOW, I'D LIKE YOU TO WELCOME OUR SPECIAL GUEST TO HELP US DEAL WITH THE GUILT... EXPERIENCED MADAM, EDITH ANDERSON.
CLAP CLAP CLAP CLAP CLAP CLAP CLAP CLAP
OKAY. EVERYONE HOLD UP YOUR TV REMOTE CONTROL AND YOUR GIN & TONIC.

COME LITTLE FISHES. COME GET YOUR FOOD!
EVE! WHEN WAS THE LAST TIME YOU CLEANED THE AQUARIUM?!!
WHAT AQUARIUM?

WATCH OUT, MOM! IT'S A PARKTOWN PRAWN!
SIZZLE SIZZLE SIZZLE!
NOW THAT'S WHAT I CALL A STRONG GIN & TONIC.

CLICK
RAINDROPS KEEP FALLIN' ON MY HEAD. BUT THAT DOESN'T MEAN MY EYES WILL SOON BE TURNIN' RED.
Raindrops keep fallin' on my head. But that doesn't mean my eyes will soon be turnin' red.
KARIOKE
10 Rand

CAUTION
MEN
WORKING

I WROTE A POEM FOR SCHOOL.
THAT'S NICE.
I CALL IT "ODE TO A GIN & TONIC."
GIN & TONIC... IT LOOKS SO BUBBLY. AND WHEN YOU DRINK IT, YOUR LEGS GO RUBBERY.
YOU READ THAT TO YOUR CLASS ?!
YEAH. MY TEACHER SAYS SHE WANTS TO HAVE A TALK WITH YOU.

AND NOW... WE CONTINUE WITH OUR TOP TWENTY GOLDEN OLDIE COUNTDOWN..
... COMING IN AT NUMBER TWELVE--
...THAT, OF COURSE, WAS THE BEACH BOYS... WITH "SURFIN' USA."

HELLO. I'M THULI, YOUR HOST ... AND I'LL BE TAKING YOU ON OUR SPECIAL TOUR OF THE UNION BUILDINGS.
LOOK MADAM! A STATUE OF DE KLERK!
OW!
AND PLEASE DON'T TOUCH THE POLITICIANS!
BLADDY TOURISTS!

OVER HERE, EVERYONE! THIS IS THE ENTRANCE TO THE CABINET ROOM. AND YOU'RE LUCKY-- CABINET IS NOW IN SESSION!
AT THIS VERY MOMENT, CRUCIAL DECISIONS ARE BEING DISCUSSED THAT WILL AFFECT THIS COUNTRY'S FUTURE. ...LISTEN!
MISTER CHAIRMAN! WE'VE BEEN ARGUING FOR HOURS. I SAY WE PUT IT TO A VOTE!
HEAR! HEAR!
YEBO!
...ALL THOSE IN FAVOUR OF CHICKEN FOR LUNCH, RAISE YOUR HAND!
NO WAY!
...PIZZA!

MADAM... I DON'T THINK IT'S SUCH A GOOD IDEA TO LEAVE THE UNION BUILDING TOUR GROUP!
I DON'T BELIEVE IT!
LOOK! IT'S HIM! RIGHT IN THE CORRIDOR! IT'S THABO M'BEKI!!!
THABO! WAIT FOR ME!!
IT'S AN HONOUR, MR. DEPUTY PRESIDENT! CAN I SHAKE YOUR HAND?!
...NOW?
MEN

MADAM! WE'RE LOST! LET'S GO BACK AND FIND THE TOUR GROUP!
LOOK! A FRAMED PICTURE OF GRACA MACHEL!
WE'RE IN THE PRESIDENT'S OFFICE!!
LOOK EVERYONE! I'M THE PRESIDENT! WE'RE FREE AT LAST!
MOM! GET OUT OF THAT CHAIR!!

MADAM! THIS IS NELSON MANDELA'S OFFICE! WE'RE NOT SUPPOSED TO BE HERE!
AND PASS UP THIS GREAT OPPOR-TUNITY?!
QUICK TAKE A PHOTO OF ME BEHIND HIS DESK.
MADAM...
HEY! HOW DID YOU GET IN HERE?!
HURRY UP! TAKE THE PICTURE!
CLICK

DO YOU LIKE **MAGIC TRICKS**?
WATCH CLOSELY! NOTHING UP MY SLEEVES! YOU WANT TO SEARCH ME?
NO.
MY FIRST TRICK IS CALLED... "THE INCREDIBLE DISAPPEARING FIFTY RAND NOTE!"
FIRST. I'LL NEED TO BORROW A FIFTY RAND NOTE.
LET'S SKIP TO THE INCREDIBLE SECOND TRICK.

GO AHEAD. PICK A CARD. ...**ANY** CARD!
NO.
WANT ME TO CHOOSE ONE **FOR YOU**?
NO.
OKAY! **REMEMBER** THIS CARD!
NO.
I WONDER IF DAVID COPPERFIELD HAS PROBLEMS LIKE THIS?
NO.

AND NOW, FOR MY NEXT TRICK, I'LL BE NEEDING A **VOLUNTEER** FROM THE AUDIENCE!
ANYONE WHO WISHES TO VOLUNTEER, SIMPLY HOLD UP A NEWSPAPER.
AND WE **HAVE** OUR VOLUNTEER! **GIVE HER A BIG HAND!**
NOW WATCH CLOSELY! FIRST I TAKE OUT A REAL LIVE **MOUSE**
NOT SO FAST.

WHAT ABOUT YOU?! DO YOU KNOW ANY MAGIC TRICKS?
SEE THIS GIN & TONIC? WATCH CLOSELY... AND I'LL MAKE IT DISAPPEAR.
THAT'S NOT A TRICK! I SEE THAT EVERY DAY!
GLUG GLUG GLUG
SOMETIMES TWICE A DAY. SOMETIMES THREE, FOUR, FIVE--
ALRIGHT! I GET THE IDEA!!

THAT'S RIGHT LADIES AND GENTLEMEN... HER CARD WAS THE ACE OF CLUBS!
BUT WHERE IS IT? IT APPEARS TO HAVE VANISHED FROM THE DECK!
BUT WAIT! INSIDE THAT GIN & TONIC! THERE'S SOMETHING ALL MUSHED UP! IT'S... IT'S...
...THE ACE OF CLUBS.
SOME PEOPLE JUST DON'T APPRECIATE MAGIC.

MADAM & Eve
BY S. FRANCIS, H. DUGMORE & RICO
From humble beginnings...
WHAT?! WE'RE OUT OF FERTILIZER ALREADY ?!
LUYT FERT
LUYT FERTILIZER
He built an empire.
THE CITIZEN
He had many enemies.
ANDRE! WHY WON'T THEY LEAVE ME ALONE?
@#%@# MEDIA!
But when they cried "Nepotism", it was time to *fight.*
WE'RE GOING TO SUE! GET MY FAMILY OUT OF THEIR OFFICES AND IN HERE NOW!
YES, UNCLE LOUIS.
Warner Bros Pictures presents
One Man's fight for freedom of speech ...and the right to hire his family.
The People vs. Louis Luyt
Starring Louis Luyt
Produced by Mrs Louis Luyt Directed by Louis Luyt Junior
Coming soon to a Theatre Near You.

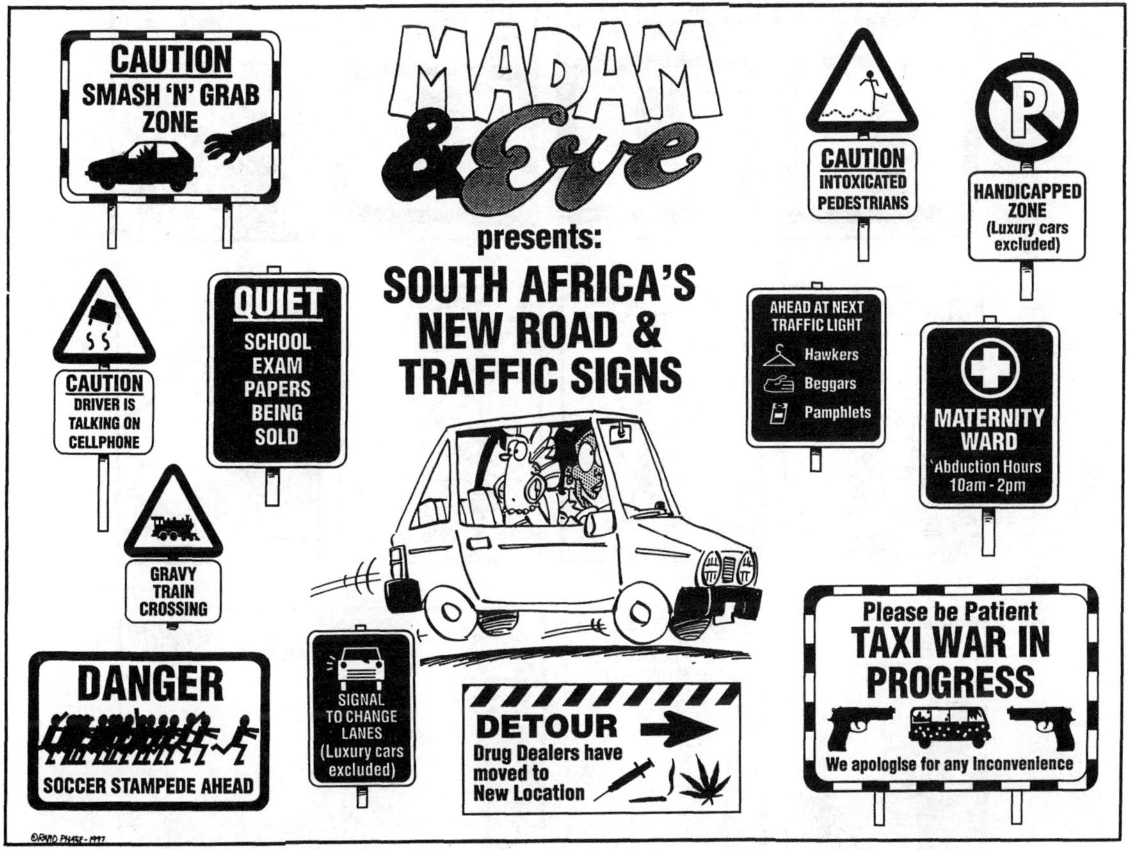

MADAM & Eve
presents:
SOUTH AFRICA'S NEW ROAD & TRAFFIC SIGNS
CAUTION
SMASH 'N' GRAB ZONE
CAUTION
INTOXICATED PEDESTRIANS
HANDICAPPED ZONE
(Luxury cars excluded)
QUIET
SCHOOL EXAM PAPERS BEING SOLD
CAUTION
DRIVER IS TALKING ON CELLPHONE
AHEAD AT NEXT TRAFFIC LIGHT
Hawkers
Beggars
Pamphlets
MATERNITY WARD
Abduction Hours 10am - 2pm
GRAVY TRAIN CROSSING
DANGER
SOCCER STAMPEDE AHEAD
SIGNAL TO CHANGE LANES
(Luxury cars excluded)
DETOUR
Drug Dealers have moved to New Location
Please be Patient
TAXI WAR IN PROGRESS
We apologise for any inconvenience
©RAPID PHASE-1997

AND IN OTHER NEWS, PRINCESS DIANA SLIPPED INTO SOUTH AFRICA THIS WEEK.
APART FROM A VISIT WITH NELSON MANDELA, DI HAS SO FAR MANAGED TO AVOID PHOTOGRAPHERS AND THE PRESS.
WHERE IS DI? NO ONE KNOWS. BUT RUMOURS PERSIST THAT SHE'S STAYING AT A PRIVATE HOME.
SO. WHAT ATTRACTED YOU TO PRINCE CHARLES?
HIS EARS.
HELLO MARGE? YOU'RE NOT GOING TO BELIEVE THIS.
GUESS WHO'S STAYING WITH US WHILE SHE'S IN SOUTH AFRICA? PRINCESS DI!
NO, I'M NOT JOKING! SHE'S IN MY LOUNGE RIGHT NOW TALKING TO EVE ABOUT SOUTH AFRICAN POLITICS AND WORLD AFFAIRS.
OKAY. CAPTAIN JAMES HEWITT... YES OR NO?
ON A SCALE FROM ONE TO TEN?
PRINCESS DI... I'D LIKE YOU TO MEET SOMEONE VERY SPECIAL...
AAAAAAH!! SHE FOUND ME!! KEEP HER AWAY!! KEEP BACK!!
THIS IS WEIRD, MOM. DI SAYS YOU LOOK EXACTLY LIKE HER MOTHER IN LAW!
REALLY? I LOOK LIKE THE QUEEN OF ENGLAND?
MY LOYAL SUBJECTS...
AAAAH!! NO! STAY BACK!

SO, LADY DI--WHAT DO YOU THINK OF SOUTH AFRICA?
I LOVE IT!
DING! DONG!
THAT COULD BE FOR ME. I'M EXPECTING SOMEONE.
DING! DONG!
I'M COMING!
DI!
FERGIE!
OH GREAT. NOW WE HAVE TO ENTERTAIN THE WHOLE FAMILY.

Le Club
EXCUSE ME.
I WAS WONDERING IF WE COULD JUMP THE QUEUE AND GO TO THE VIP SECTION.
AND WHO DO YOU THINK YOU ARE? THE QUEEN OF ENGLAND?
ACTUALLY, YES. I AM ... AND THIS IS PRINCESS DIANA AND FERGIE.
GASP
I CAN'T BELIEVE IT! DI AND FERGIE IN OUR CLUB!
THAT'S NOTHING. LOOK AT THE QUEEN OF ENGLAND PUT AWAY THOSE GIN & TONICS!

AND IN OTHER NEWS, THABO MBEKI'S HOUSE WAS BURGLED THIS WEEK. THIEVES TOOK APPLIANCES, A HI-FI, AND VALUABLE CAMERA EQUIPMENT.
IS NO ONE SAFE IN THIS COUNTRY?! NOT EVEN THE DEPUTY PRESIDENT!!
MISTER MBEKI SAYS HE'S IN THE PROCESS OF DOING A COMPLETE AUDIT TO DETERMINE EXACTLY WHAT WAS STOLEN.
MY KENNY G CD'S!! THEY TOOK MY KENNY G CD'S!!
WE'RE INSURED, THABO. COME TO BED.

THABO MBEKI'S HOUSE WAS BURGLED?! WHAT IS THIS COUNTRY COMING TO?
COULD YOU SIGN THIS, MR. PRESIDENT?
WHAT AM I SIGNING? AN ORDER TO BEEF UP SECURITY?
NO. AN AUTOGRAPH FOR MY BROTHER.
DO I KNOW YOU?
NOT REALLY. I JUST WALKED IN THROUGH THE FRONT DOOR.
SECURITY!!
THEY'RE ON A BREAK. COULD YOU MAKE IT OUT... "TO BOB?"

HELP! SECURITY!!
YES, MISTER PRESIDENT?
NO WONDER THABO MBEKI'S HOUSE WAS BURGLED! THIS MAN JUST WALKED INTO MY OFFICE TO GET AN AUTOGRAPH FOR HIS BROTHER!
YOU'RE NOT SECURITY, ARE YOU?
I'M HIS BROTHER. THE AUTOGRAPH'S FOR ME.
DIDN'T I TELL YOU TO WAIT IN THABO MBEKI'S OFFICE!

OKAY. WHAT'S THE EMER- GENCY?
IT'S THABO MBEKI, MISTER PRESIDENT! SINCE HE'S BEEN BURGLED, HE REFUSES TO LEAVE HIS HOUSE!
THABO! ARE YOU IN THERE?
WHO WANTS TO KNOW?
CAN'T YOU RECOGNISE MY VOICE?!
JEREMY MANSFIELD?
I'M THE REAL PRESIDENT, DAMMIT!
SLIDE SOME I.D. UNDER THE DOOR!

READY, MR. PRESIDENT? ...PICTURE THIS: LANDMINES!
NO WAY.
AN ELECTRIFIED DOOR-BELL! ONE PUSH... AND ZAP! 2000 VOLTS AND THEY'RE HISTORY!
I DON'T THINK SO.
GIANT REVOLVING AUTOMATIC GUN TURRETS ON THE ROOF?
THABO-- I KNOW I AGREED TO BEEF UP SECURITY AROUND YOUR HOUSE, BUT...
WAIT! I HAVEN'T TOLD YOU ABOUT THE EXPLODING STOEP YET!

MADAM & Eve
BY S.FRANCIS, H.DUGMORE & RICO
I JUST LOVE FLEA MARKETS. THERE'S NO TELLING WHAT BARGAINS YOU'LL FIND!
HI. COULD I INTEREST YOU IN SOMETHING FROM THABO MBEKI'S HOUSE?
WHAT?!
JUST LOOK AT THIS STEREO HI-FI! THABO LOVED THIS! ONLY 599-99!
IN FACT, HE USED TO LISTEN TO IT WHILE HE SMOKED HIS PIPE...
...ACTUALLY THIS VERY PIPE. ...24-99.
OR...HOW ABOUT A WALL CLOCK... DIRECT FROM CHIEF BUTHELEZI'S LOUNGE?!
...A PEN AND PENCIL SET FROM NELSON MANDELA'S PRIVATE OFFICE?? FOR YOU -- ONLY THREE HUNDRED RAND!
ARE YOU CRAZY?! ALL THIS MERCHANDISE IS STOLEN!
OKAY! OKAY! ...TWO-HUNDRED RAND!
THAT DOES IT!! WE'RE GOING TO FIND A POLICEMAN!
NO NEED! I HAVE SEVERAL RIGHT HERE!
WAIT! COME BACK! YOU WANT A SERGEANT OR A CAPTAIN ?!!

MADAM & Eve
CASABLANCA
Starring
Humphrey Boesak
BY S. FRANCIS, H. DUGMORE & RICO
ALLAN-- WE'VE GOT TO GET ON THAT PLANE!
FORGET IT SWEETHEART! I'M NOT GOING.
BUT ALLAN! IF YOU STAY IN SOUTH AFRICA... THEY'LL ARREST YOU! THEY'LL PUT YOU ON TRIAL!
PUT ME ON TRIAL ?! ...WHEN I GO ON TRIAL... THE STRUGGLE FOR JUSTICE GOES ON TRIAL!
...WHEN I GO ON TRIAL, THE STRUGGLE FOR FREEDOM GOES ON TRIAL. WHEN I GO ON TRIAL, ALL MY PEOPLE GO ON TRIAL!
FOR FRAUD?
THE ENGINES ARE STARTING. YOU BETTER GO.
OH ALLAN.
HEY! MY WALLET'S GONE!
HERE'S LOOKING AT YOU, KID.
DID SOMEONE MENTION A MISSING WALLET?
CHIEF OMAR!
ROUND UP THE USUAL SUSPECTS!
YES SIR.
CHIEF... THIS LOOKS LIKE THE BEGINNING OF A BEAUTIFUL FRIENDSHIP.

HOW'S MY MOTHER, DOCTOR?
OH, SHE'S FINE.
...EXCEPT... IT'S THE STRANGEST THING. HER BLOOD PRESSURE JUMPS EVERY FEW SECONDS.
MIELLLIES!
SEE? THERE IT GOES AGAIN?

I HATE BEING IN HOSPITAL.
HELLO. THEY TOLD ME YOU'D BE ARRIVING TODAY.
WHO THE HELL ARE YOU?
I'M YOUR SISTER.
NOT FROM MY SIDE OF THE FAMILY.

WE HAVE TO TAKE YOUR TEMPERATURE EVERY DAY WHILE YOU'RE IN HOSPITAL, MRS. ANDERSON. NOW PLEASE--OPEN UP.
HEH-HEH. NO WAY.
BY THE WAY, I HEAR YOU LIKE GIN & TONIC.
WHY, YES! I USUALLY--
OOOOOH. SHE'S SO TRICKY.

I WANT MY DOCTOR!! I WANT MY DOCTOR!!
HELLO. I'M YOUR DOCTOR. CAN I HELP YOU?
I WANT A SECOND OPINION!! I WANT A SECOND OPINION!!

HI MOM.
GWEN! THANKS FOR VISITING ME IN HOSPITAL!
COME ON! LET'S TAKE A WALK. I WANT TO GIVE A MESSAGE TO ALL THE HOSPITAL STAFF.
MOM! THE BACK OF YOUR GOWN IS OPEN! EVERYONE CAN SEE YOUR BUM!
I KNOW. THAT'S THE MESSAGE.

GOOD MORNING! AND HOW ARE WE FEELING TODAY?
WE?!! THERE'S NO "WE." IT'S JUST ME. I'M THE ONE THAT'S IN THE HOSPITAL! I'M THE ONE YOU WAKE UP AT FIVE IN THE MORNING! I'M THE ONE WHO GETS ALL THE INJECTIONS! NOT "WE"... ME!!! GET IT ?!!
MY. WE'RE A LITTLE UPSET TODAY, AREN'T WE ?

ARE YOU FINISHED?
YES. AND ALWAYS REMEMBER, SISTER...
AN OPTIMIST SEES THE GLASS AS HALF FULL, A PESSIMIST SEES IT AS HALF EMPTY.
I HATE ASKING HER FOR A URINE SAMPLE.

ATCHOO!!
HONK!!
GOOD MORNING! THE DOCTOR SAYS HE WANTS A TISSUE SAMPLE TODAY.
HERE YOU GO. ALL YOURS.

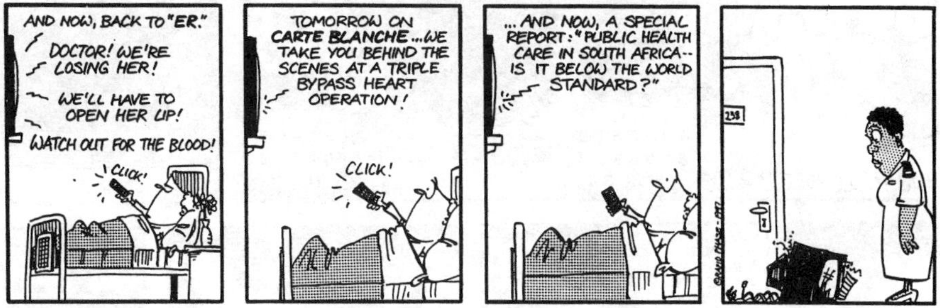
AND NOW, BACK TO "ER."
DOCTOR! WE'RE LOSING HER!
WE'LL HAVE TO OPEN HER UP!
WATCH OUT FOR THE BLOOD!
CLICK!
TOMORROW ON CARTE BLANCHE ...WE TAKE YOU BEHIND THE SCENES AT A TRIPLE BYPASS HEART OPERATION!
CLICK!
... AND NOW, A SPECIAL REPORT: "PUBLIC HEALTH CARE IN SOUTH AFRICA-- IS IT BELOW THE WORLD STANDARD?"
238

IT'S COCKTAIL HOUR, EDITH. I BROUGHT US TWO ICE COLD GIN & TONICS.
BE RIGHT BACK-- I'M JUST GETTING THE CHIPS & DIP.
GIN & TONIC?!! WHAT WOULD YOUR DOCTOR SAY ABOUT THAT?!
THAT IS MY DOCTOR.

MADAM & Eve
BY S. FRANCIS, H. DUGMORE & RICO
KLOMP! KLOMP! KLOMP!
SUBJECT SPOTTED AT UNION BUILDINGS. COMMENCE OPERATION "GIN & TONIC."
WUPWUPWUPWUP!
WUPWUP WUPWUP WUP!
IT'S WORKING, SIR. SHE'S TAKING THE BAIT!
WUPWUPWUPWUPWUP!!
KLOMP! KLOMP!
MIELLLIES!!
OH NO! IT'S ANOTHER ONE!
KLOMP! KLOMP! KLOMP!
KLOMP! KLOMP! KLOMP!
MIELLLIES!!
AAARGH!
WHAT WAS MOM WATCHING BEFORE SHE FELL ASLEEP?
SOME JAPANESE MONSTER MOVIE... WHY?

MADAM & Eve
BY S.FRANCIS, H.DUGMORE & RICO
TARGET SIGHTED. TORPEDO ONE... FIRE!!
MIELLLIES!
MOM! I THOUGHT I BOUGHT THAT TELESCOPE SO YOU COULD WATCH THE HALE-BOPP COMET!!
SIGH
SEE ANYTHING YET, MOM ?!
NOT YET.
WAIT A MINUTE! I SEE SOMETHING! I THINK IT'S ... A BIG PLANET!
AND THIS IS INCREDIBLE!! I'VE FOUND A BLACK HOLE!
HOLD IT! I THINK I SEE THE COMET! YES! IT'S... YELLOW! AND YOU'RE NOT GOING TO BELIEVE THIS -- IT LOOKS LIKE... LIKE... A GIANT MIELIE!!
... GIANT MIELIE ?!!
CAN YOU STILL SEE THEM?
YES. YOUR MOTHER'S GAINING.

WHUPWHUPWHUPWHUPWHUP
ZZZZIP!!
WHUP WHUP WHUP WHUP..
THWAK!!
HEH-HEH. I'LL BET THAT'S WHY THEY DON'T HAVE ANY MIELIE LADIES IN AUSTRALIA.

MIRROR MIRROR ON THE WALL... WHO'S THE BEST MAID OF THEM ALL?
THAT'S NOT A MIRROR. THAT'S A WINDOW THAT HASN'T BEEN CLEANED FOR THREE MONTHS.
I LIKED IT BETTER AS A MIRROR.

YOU'RE RIGHT. THAT IS THE SMALLEST CELLPHONE I'VE EVER SEEN.

HOLLYWOOD VERSION
Arnold Schwarzenegger in
THE TERMINATOR
I'LL BE BACK.
SOUTH AFRICAN VERSION
Arnold Schwarzenegger in
THE EMIGRATOR
I WON'T BE BACK.

DOMESTIC FLIGHTS ONLY

TO EACH HIS OWN
Only 10 Rand
OKAY. HERE'S MY TEN BUCKS. WHAT DO I GET?
NOTHING.
TO EACH HIS OWN
WHAT?! I GET NOTHING?! THAT'S THE BIGGEST RIP-OFF I EVER HEARD OF!!
HEY- TO EACH HIS OWN.
TO EACH HIS OWN
TO EACH HIS OWN
Only 10 Rand

WILL THE **SPECIAL EDITION** OF THE **TRUTH AND RECONCILIATION COMMISSION** PLEASE COME TO ORDER!
BANG!
OUR FIRST WITNESS IS SEEKING **AMNESTY** FOR BLOWING UP ENTIRE **SOLAR SYSTEMS** AND **PLANETS** OVER TWENTY YEARS AGO.
THE TRUTH COMMISSION CALLS MR. VADER. IS **DARTH VADER** HERE?
I WAS ONLY FOLLOWING ORDERS.
SURE. THAT'S WHAT THEY **ALL** SAY.

SO, **MR VADER**, YOU **ADMIT** YOU TRIED TO **CRUSH** THE **REBEL FORCES** BY BUILDING THE **DEATH STAR** FOR THE **EMPIRE**!
YES.
THAT WAS OVER TWENTY YEARS AGO. WHY COME FORWARD TO THE TRUTH COMMISSION **NOW**?
BECAUSE, I'M NOT THE **SAME MAN** I WAS TWENTY YEARS AGO.
YOU MEAN...
YES. I'VE BEEN **DIGITALLY ENHANCED**, **REMIXED** AND TOTALLY **REMASTERED**.
SEE? PEOPLE CAN CHANGE!

MR. VADER! YOU BLEW UP ENTIRE PLANETS! HOW CAN THIS TRUTH COMMISSION POSSIBLY GRANT YOU AMNESTY?!!
CHOKE! GHACK!
PLOP!
I VOTE FOR AMNESTY!
I SECOND IT!

THE SPECIAL EDITION TRUTH COMMISSION CALLS THE NEXT WITNESS SEEKING AMNESTY... **LUKE SKYWALKER.**
MR. SKYWALKER... IT'S ALLEGED YOU BLEW UP THE DEATH STAR. WHAT WE NEED TO KNOW IS **WHERE** DID IT HAPPEN... AND **WHEN**?
CAN I CONSULT WITH MY ATTORNEY?
BSSST. BSSST.
BEEP. BEEP. BOOOP! DAWHEEP!
...A LONG TIME AGO IN A GALAXY FAR FAR AWAY.
SPECIFICS! WE WANT **SPECIFICS!**

THE TRUTH COMMISSION IS GETTING IMPATIENT MR. SKYWALKER.
WHAT WAS THE QUESTION, AGAIN?
WHEN YOU **BLEW UP** THE DEATH STAR AND DEFEATED THE EMPIRE... DID YOU DO IT **ALONE**?!
NO. **THE FORCE** WAS WITH ME.
THE FORCE?!
AHA! THE **THIRD** FORCE!! **NOW** WE'RE GETTING **SOMEWHERE!**

A long time ago
In a supermarket
far, far away...
SPAR WARS
SPECIAL 1-17
FLOUR RICE
FROZEN FISH

MADAM & EVE
SPECIAL EDITION
DIGITALLY REMASTERED COMPUTER ENHANCED
SIX TRACK DOLBY SOUND
BY S.FRANCIS, H.DUGMORE & RICO
A long time ago
In a suburb far, far away...
FORGIVE ME FATHER FOR I HAVE SINNED. FOR YEARS I'VE BEEN PAYING MY MAID EVE ONLY 10 RAND FOR A FULL DAY'S WORK.
I SEE...
...IS SHE AVAILABLE TUESDAYS?
EVE, I FEEL TERRIBLE... THERE MUST BE SOMETHING I CAN DO TO EASE THE GUILT I FEEL OVER ONLY PAYING YOU TEN RAND A DAY.
WHAT IF...? NO... IT PROBABLY WOULD NOT WORK...
WHAT?!... TELL ME!!
WHAT IF... YOU ACTUALLY... PAID ME MORE?
PAY YOU MORE?
YES! THAT'S A BRILLIANT IDEA, EVE... A NEW TYPE OF RADICAL GUILT THERAPY!
I'LL GET MY PURSE.
BETTER MAKE IT YOUR CHEQUE-BOOK! WE'RE DEALING WITH A LOT OF GUILT HERE!
©Rapid Phase Productions 1992

MADAM & Eve
BY S. FRANCIS, H. DUGMORE & RICO
I KNOW! LET'S PLAY A GAME! LET'S PLAY COPS & ROBBERS!!
I'M THE ROBBER!
NO WAY! I'M THE ROBBER!
HEY! I WANT TO BE THE ROBBER!!
WELL! THINGS HAVE CERTAINLY CHANGED... WHEN I WAS YOUR AGE, EVERYONE WANTED TO BE A COP!
ARE YOU CRAZY?! COPS WORK LONG HOURS FOR HARDLY ANY MONEY!
...RESULTING IN DEPRESSION AND DIVORCE.
BANK ROBBERS MAKE LOTS OF MONEY!
THEIR HOURS ARE FLEXIBLE AND THEY'RE SELF-EMPLOYED!
...AND ONLY 10% OF THEM EVER GET CAUGHT!
...AND EVEN IF THEY DO GET CAUGHT, IT'S REAL EASY TO GET OUT ON BAIL--
OKAY! OKAY! FORGET I EVEN ASKED! BESIDES... DON'T YOU KNOW ANY OTHER GAMES?
I KNOW! LET'S PLAY... "PUBLIC PROTECTORS AND CORRUPT GOVERNMENT OFFICIALS!"
I'M THE CORRUPT OFFICIAL!
NO WAY! I'M THE CORRUPT OFFICIAL!!
HEY! I WANT TO BE THE CORRUPT OFFICIAL!

WITHDRAWALS
BLAM! BLAM! BLAM!
OKAY! EVERYONE ON THE FLOOR!! THIS IS A BANK ROBBERY!!
HEY! WAIT IN THE QUEUE LIKE EVERYONE ELSE, YOUNG MAN!
COULD YOU PLEASE KEEP IT DOWN?!! I'M TRYING TO GET A LOAN APPROVED HERE!!
YOU KNOW, MADAM... I THINK PEOPLE ARE GETTING TOO USED TO ALL THESE BANK ROBBERIES.
"GET ON THE FLOOR?!" THESE ARE MY NEW PANTS!
I DON'T KNOW WHY I COME TO THIS BANK! THEY ONLY GIVE ME 14% ON A FIXED DEPOSIT!
EXCUSE ME..., BUT THE BANK DOWN THE STREET GIVES 16,5% ON FIXED DEPOSITS.
16,5?? REALLY?!
HEY! I SAID NO TALKING UNTIL WE'RE FINISHED!
BA

HOW'S THIS?
GOOD. READY?
WAIT A MINUTE! YOU'RE ALWAYS IN THE PHOTO! HERE. TAKE ONE OF ME!
FINE!
OKAY. BIG SMILE.
THESE BANK ROBBERS JUST GET BOLDER AND BOLDER.

FREEZE! POLICE!!
THANK GOODNESS. THE POLICE.
HEY PIET! OUR VOLUNTARY RETRENCHMENT PACKAGES WERE JUST APPROVED!
REALLY?!!
HERE. HOLD THIS.
I HATE IT WHEN THEY DO THAT.

BANK

AND IN OTHER NEWS, WINNIE MANDELA IS SELLING BOTTLES OF SOIL FROM HER BACK YARD TO COMMEMORATE WHERE THE STRUGGLE BEGAN. THE PRICE IS FIFTY RAND PER BOTTLE AND THEY ARE SELLING WELL...
WINNIE'S MAKING A FORTUNE SELLING SOIL TO TOURISTS! CAN YOU BELIEVE THAT, MOM ?!!
©RAPID PHASE-1997 kardug@iafrica.co.za
ARE YOU SURE THIS TAXI GOES TO SOWETO ?
SOWETAN

LOOK OLGA, A BOTTLE OF SOIL FROM WINNIE MANDELA'S BACK YARD.
JA, AND WE GOT IT AT HALF PRICE!
©RAPID PHASE-1997 kardug@iafrica.co.za
CELEBRITY SOIL
DIRECT FROM THEIR BACK YARD!
Only 25 Rand

CELEBRITY SOIL
DIRECT FROM THEIR BACK YARD!
Only 25 Rand
EVE, YOU CAN'T SELL SOIL FROM OUR OWN BACK YARD AND SAY IT'S FROM WINNIE'S HOUSE!
MAYBE THIS IS FROM WINNIE'S HOUSE.
...MAYBE MY PARTNER AND I WENT THERE OURSELVES AND DUG IT UP.
©RAPID PHASE 1997 kardug@iafrica.co.za
PARTNER?! WHAT PARTNER?!!
GOT ANOTHER LOAD. COMING THROUGH HERE.

MARGE, I'M WORRIED ABOUT EVE AND MY MOTHER.
WHY?
I THINK THEY'RE SELLING SOIL FROM WINNIE MANDELA'S HOUSE TO TOURISTS.
WHAT? HOW?!
I'M NOT SURE, BUT THEY ALWAYS SEEM TO HAVE PLENTY OF MERCHANDISE.
FINALLY. WINNIE'S GONE TO BED.
GOOD. YOU CARRY THE BUCKETS, I'LL GET THE SHOVELS.

HEY!! WHO'S OUT THERE?!!
UH-OH.
WINNIE, SOMEONE'S STEALING YOUR SOIL AGAIN!
THIS SOIL BELONGS TO THE PEOPLE!!
THAT DOES IT! I'M GETTING A SOIL BODYGUARD!!
OW! YOU'RE STANDING ON MY FACE!

MADAM & Eve
BY S.FRANCIS, H.DUGMORE & RICO
WILL THIS FAMILY AMNESTY APPLICATION HEARING NOW COME TO ORDER!
BONK!
OKAY. WHO WANTS TO CONFESS FIRST?
I'LL GO FIRST. I ADMIT... THAT I MAY HAVE PAID EVE A LOWER WAGE THAN SHE DESERVES.
GOOD! ...EVE?
AND I ADMIT THAT I MAY HAVE ACCIDENTALLY BROKEN MADAM'S FAVOURITE VASE.
WHAT?! THAT WAS YOU?!
REMEMBER - AMNESTY, GWEN! AMNESTY!!
GO ON. YOUR TURN.
I ADMIT THAT... I MAY HAVE BEEN WRONG NOT TO GIVE EVE PAID LEAVE WHEN HER UNCLE JOE WAS SICK.
...EVE?
AND I ADMIT I MAY HAVE BEEN WRONG TO SAY MY "UNCLE JOE" WAS SICK... WHEN I DON'T EVEN HAVE AN UNCLE JOE.
WHAT?! YOU MADE IT UP?!!
AMNESTY, GWEN! ...AMNESTY!!
EASY FOR YOU TO SAY, MOM! NONE OF THIS AFFECTS YOU!
ER, THAT'S NOT EXACTLY TRUE. YOU KNOW THOSE GIN & TONICS I BRING HER EVERY NIGHT?
YES...
WHENEVER SHE YELLED AT ME, I MAY HAVE STIRRED THEM WITH MY FINGER.
©RAPID PHASE 1997 hardug@iafrica.co.za
AMNESTY, MOM! AMNESTY!!

MADAM & Eve
BY S.FRANCIS, H.DUGMORE & RICO
...AND IN OTHER NEWS, THE RESULT OF THE ANC WOMEN'S LEAGUE PRESIDENTIAL ELECTION ARE FINALLY IN. THE WINNER IS... WINNIE MADIKIZELA MANDELA!
GROAN
SIGH
AARRGH!
OKAY. WHO-EVER PICKS THE SHORT STRAW HAS TO TELL YOU-KNOW-WHO.
COME IN.
KNOCK KNOCK
MORNING, MISTER PRESIDENT.
GOOD MORNING!
HEY--HOW ABOUT BAFANA BAFANA? DID YOU SEE THE GAME?
YES. BUT I'M UH, RATHER BUSY RIGHT NOW...
THEN LET ME GET TO THE POINT, SIR. I HAVE GOOD NEWS AND BAD NEWS.
WHICH DO YOU WANT FIRST?
THE BAD NEWS.
...YOUR EX-WIFE WAS JUST ELECTED PRESIDENT OF THE ANC WOMEN'S LEAGUE.
QUICKLY! WHAT'S THE GOOD NEWS?
IT COULD HAVE BEEN DOCTOR ZUMA!
SIR?... MISTER PRESIDENT? ARE YOU OKAY?... SIR?

RELAX MOM. IT LOOKS LIKE WE'RE GOING TO BE STUCK IN TRAFFIC FOR A... A...
OH NO. NOT AGAIN.
...WHAT??
I'M TELLING YOU, MOM! THESE ARE THE SAME THREE GUYS THAT I ALWAYS GET STUCK BEHIND IN TRAFFIC! THEY'RE CRAZY!!
THEY LOOK NORMAL ENOUGH TO ME.
THERE!! DID YOU SEE THAT?!!
SEE WHAT?
LEAVE US ALONE! STOP STARING AT US!
DON'T LET THEM INTIMIDATE YOU! JUST STARE RIGHT BACK!
THOSE GUYS ARE GOOD.
DON'T BLINK!

OH NO! WITH ALL THIS TRAFFIC MY ENGINE'S OVERHEATED!!
WELL?! INSTEAD OF STARING, WHY DON'T THE THREE OF YOU DO SOMETHING?!!

IT'S STRANGE, DOCTOR. EVERY DAY IN MY CAR I GET STUCK BEHIND THESE THREE BLACK GUYS IN A TRUCK.
GO ON...
IT'S ALMOST LIKE... THEY'RE FOLLOWING ME! WHEREVER I GO, THEY GO!!
WHAT DO YOU THINK?
ACUTE PARANOIA.
DEFINITELY.

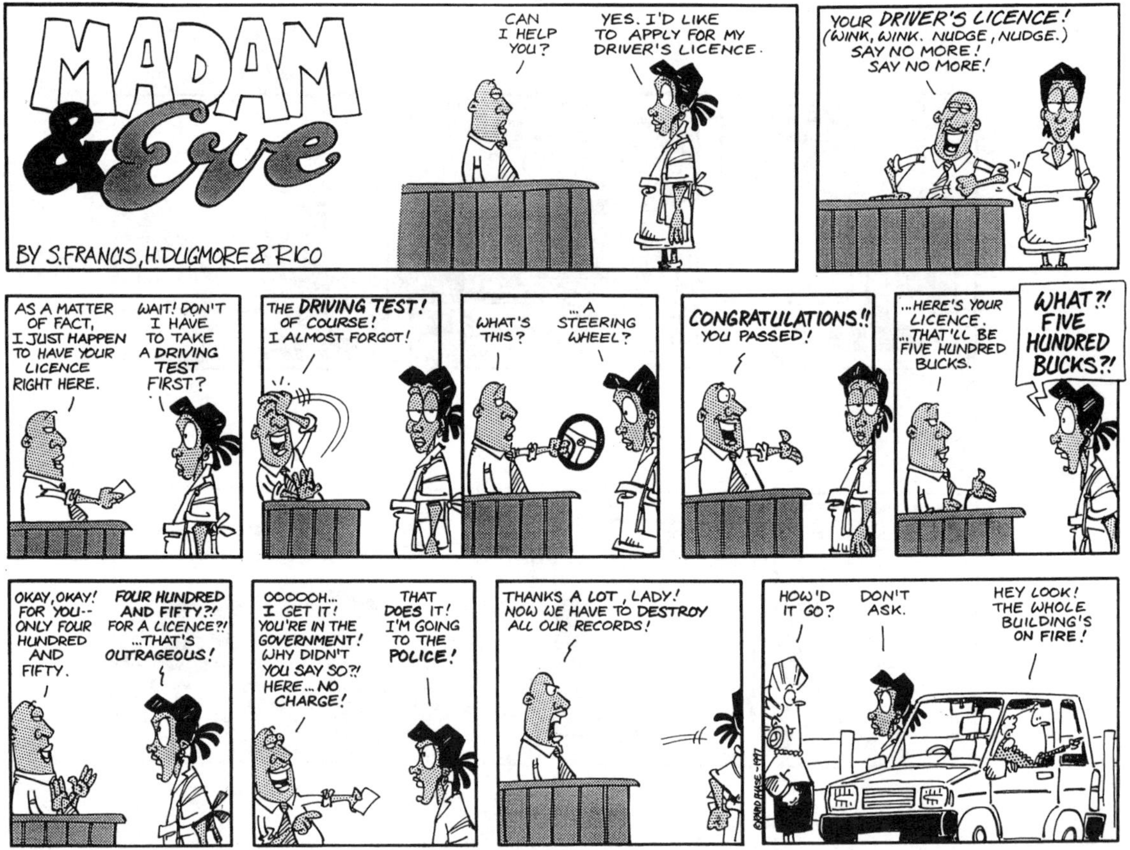
MADAM & Eve
BY S.FRANCIS, H.DUGMORE & RICO
CAN I HELP YOU?
YES. I'D LIKE TO APPLY FOR MY DRIVER'S LICENCE.
YOUR DRIVER'S LICENCE! (WINK, WINK. NUDGE, NUDGE.) SAY NO MORE! SAY NO MORE!
AS A MATTER OF FACT, I JUST HAPPEN TO HAVE YOUR LICENCE RIGHT HERE.
WAIT! DON'T I HAVE TO TAKE A DRIVING TEST FIRST?
THE DRIVING TEST! OF COURSE! I ALMOST FORGOT!
WHAT'S THIS?
...A STEERING WHEEL?
CONGRATULATIONS!! YOU PASSED!
...HERE'S YOUR LICENCE. ...THAT'LL BE FIVE HUNDRED BUCKS.
WHAT?! FIVE HUNDRED BUCKS?!
OKAY, OKAY! FOR YOU-- ONLY FOUR HUNDRED AND FIFTY.
FOUR HUNDRED AND FIFTY?! FOR A LICENCE?! ...THAT'S OUTRAGEOUS!
OOOOOH... I GET IT! YOU'RE IN THE GOVERNMENT! WHY DIDN'T YOU SAY SO?! HERE... NO CHARGE!
THAT DOES IT! I'M GOING TO THE POLICE!
THANKS A LOT, LADY! NOW WE HAVE TO DESTROY ALL OUR RECORDS!
HOW'D IT GO?
DON'T ASK.
HEY LOOK! THE WHOLE BUILDING'S ON FIRE!

MADAM & Eve
BY S.FRANCIS, H.DUGMORE & RICO
BEER PLEASE.
HEY BUDDY. WE DON'T ALLOW DOGS IN THIS PUB.
THAT'S OKAY. THIS DOG IS SPECIAL. HE'S A TALKING DOG.
...OF COURSE, IF YOU DON'T BELIEVE ME, PERHAPS YOU'D LIKE TO PUT A LITTLE WAGER ON IT.
YOU'RE ON.
FIFTY BUCKS SAYS YOUR DOG CAN'T TALK.
COUNT ME IN.
ME TOO.
OKAY BOY. ANSWER THIS QUESTION: WHAT POLITICIAN IN THE NEWS IS CAUSING HUGE PROBLEMS FOR THE NATIONAL PARTY?
ROELF!
ROELF!
ROELF!
ROELF!
ROELF!
SEE? ..."ROELF MEYER."
BONK! BONK!
OOF!
THAT DOES IT! NEXT TIME I'M GOING TO ANSWER "DE KLERK."

STICK EM UP!!
DO YOU TAKE COMPANY CREDIT CARDS?
OH... AND BY THE WAY, COULD YOU GIVE ME A RECEIPT? THAT WAY I CAN CLAIM THIS AS A LEGITIMATE BUSINESS EXPENSE PAID FOR BY THE TAXPAYER.
©RAPID PHASE-1997 hardug@iafrica.co.za
JUST GREAT. YOU HAD TO MUG AN IBA OFFICIAL.
HERE. YOU CAN USE MY PEN.

THIS MEETING OF THE IBA WILL NOW COME TO ORDER.
THE FIRST SUBJECT ON TONIGHT'S AGENDA... "OUR BUDGET: ARE WE NEEDLESSLY OVER-SPENDING TAXPAYER'S MONEY?"
CHAMPAGNE AND CAVIAR, SIR?
WHY THANK YOU, JEEVES.
©RAPID PHASE-1997 hardug@iafrica.co.za
HEY! I ASKED FOR A DOM PERIGNON '59! THIS IS ONLY A '67!
SORRY SIR. I'LL RE-CHECK THE CELLAR.

IT'S NOT FAIR! SO WE CHARGED A FEW EXTRAS ON OUR IBA CREDIT CARDS! BIG DEAL!
YOU CALL THESE BUSINESS EXPENSES?! TOYS... LIQUOR... CONCERT TICKETS... MASSAGE PARLOURS...
MASSAGE PARLOURS?!! HOW COULD THAT POSSIBLY BE AN IBA BUSINESS EXPENSE??!!
©RAPID PHASE-1997 hardug@iafrica.co.za
I'M THINKING OF STARTING UP MY OWN RADIO STATION.
PAT PAT PAT PAT PAT PAT

LADIES AND GENTLEMEN, I THINK IT'S CLEAR THAT MANY OF YOU HAVE BEEN USING IBA CREDIT CARDS FOR PERSONAL USE.
THEREFORE, UNTIL FURTHER NOTICE, I'M CONFISCATING ALL YOUR CREDIT CARDS. HAND THEM OVER.
I CAN'T.
WHAT?!!
MY WIFE BORROWED MINE TO GO SHOPPING.
Le House of Fashion
HEY PIERRE-- LOOK! AN IBA CREDIT CARD!
SACRE BLEU!

HONEY?! HAVE YOU SEEN MY IBA CREDIT CARD SLIPS?
NO DEAR. WHY?
IT'S A PROBLEM! WITHOUT THOSE SLIPS, I CAN'T PROVE THAT MY PURCHASES WERE BUSINESS AND NOT PERSONAL.
HAVE YOU CHECKED OUR DOG?
REX! BAD DOG!! YOU ATE ALL MY IBA CREDIT CARD SLIPS!
AND THAT'S WHAT HAPPENED. HONEST.
MISTER CHAIRMAN!
MISTER CHAIRMAN!

MADAM--ARE YOU THROWING OUT THIS OLD TYPEWRITER?
YES. WHY?
I'LL TAKE IT! I'VE ALWAYS WONDERED IF I COULD WRITE THE GREAT SOUTH AFRICAN NOVEL.
HEE-HEE. THE GREAT SOUTH AFRICAN NOVEL.
THIS I GOTTA SEE.
©RAPID PHASE-1997 http://www.mg.co.za/mg/
"THE MADAM FROM HELL" An unauthorised Biography

I'LL BE BACK SOON. I'M GOING TO THE SHOP. I'M OUT OF PAPER.
STILL WORKING ON THE GREAT SOUTH AFRICAN NOVEL, I SEE.
YEP. SHE'S BEEN TYPING ALL NIGHT.
©RAPID PHASE-1997 http://www.mg.co.za/mg/
"MAID TO ORDER" ...THE STORY OF A DOMESTIC WORKER AND HER GROSSLY UNFAIR EMPLOYER."
I'LL KILL HER.

I CAN'T BELIEVE EVE'S WRITING A NOVEL ABOUT US! DID SHE USE OUR REAL NAMES?
NOT EXACTLY.
...INSTEAD OF GWEN, THE MADAM'S NAME IS GWINITH. INSTEAD OF EVE, THE MAID'S NAME IS "EVA".
IS THERE A MOTHER FROM ENGLAND IN THE BOOK? WHAT'S HER NAME?
©RAPID PHASE-1997 http://www.mg.co.za/mg/
GINNY.
I'LL KILL HER.

"MAID TO ORDER" ... THE STORY OF A DOMESTIC WORKER AND HER GROSSLY UNFAIR EMPLOYER."
Chapter Twelve:
TIC TIC TIC TIC TIC
HOW DARE YOU WRITE A NOVEL ABOUT ME AND MY MOTHER WITHOUT ASKING OUR PERMISSION ?!!
©RAPID PHASE-1997 http://www.mg.co.za/mg/
Chapter Twelve: "I am discovered."
TIC TIC TIC TIC TIC

LET ME GET THIS STRAIGHT. YOU SEARCHED MY ROOM SO YOU COULD SECRETLY READ THE NOVEL I'M WRITING?
THAT'S RIGHT!
AND IT'S A GOOD THING I DID! YOU PORTRAY MY CHARACTER AS A SELFISH AND SELF-ABSORBED MADAM WHO'S SO PETTY AND CHEAP THAT SHE --
...THAT SHE...
©RAPID PHASE-1997 http://www.mg.co.za/mg/
HEY! DID YOU BUY THAT COFFEE AND SUGAR ?!!

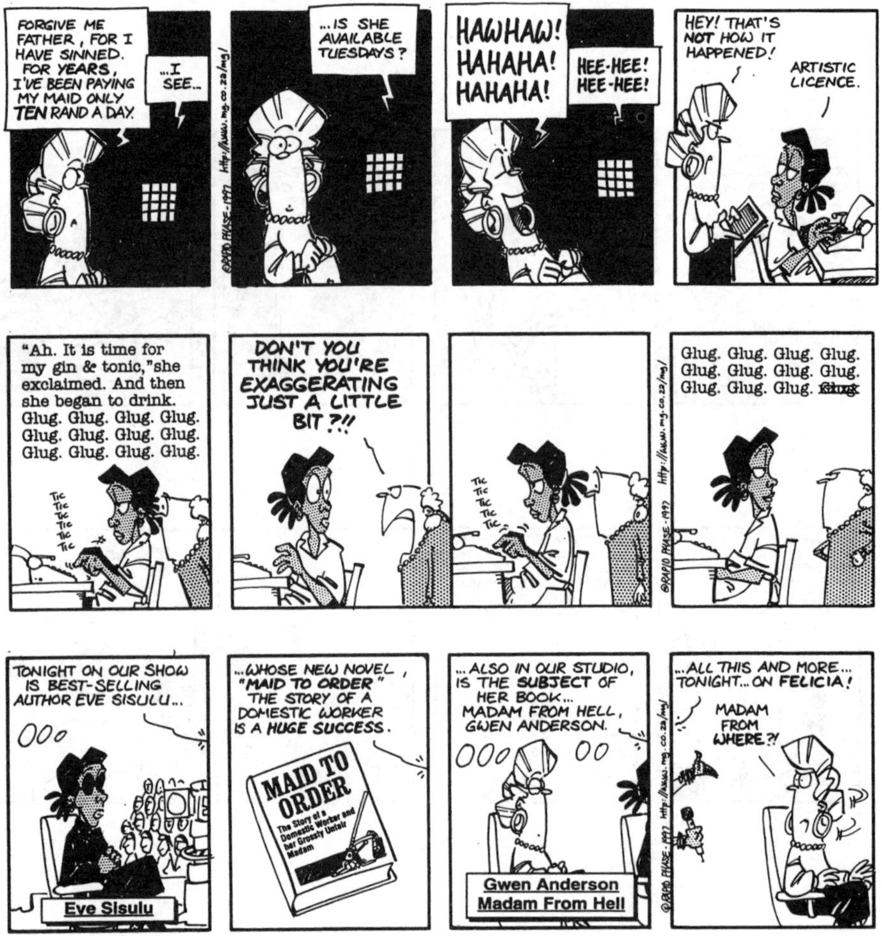
FORGIVE ME FATHER, FOR I HAVE SINNED. FOR YEARS, I'VE BEEN PAYING MY MAID ONLY TEN RAND A DAY.
...I SEE..
...IS SHE AVAILABLE TUESDAYS?
HAWHAW! HAHAHA! HAHAHA!
HEE-HEE! HEE-HEE!
HEY! THAT'S NOT HOW IT HAPPENED!
ARTISTIC LICENCE.
"Ah. It is time for my gin & tonic," she exclaimed. And then she began to drink. Glug. Glug. Glug. Glug. Glug. Glug. Glug. Glug. Glug. Glug. Glug. Glug.
TIC TIC TIC TIC TIC TIC
DON'T YOU THINK YOU'RE EXAGGERATING JUST A LITTLE BIT?!!
TIC TIC TIC TIC TIC
Glug. Glug. Glug. Glug. Glug. Glug. Glug. Glug. Glug. Glug. Glug. Glug.
TONIGHT ON OUR SHOW IS BEST-SELLING AUTHOR EVE SISULU...
Eve Sisulu
...WHOSE NEW NOVEL, "MAID TO ORDER" THE STORY OF A DOMESTIC WORKER IS A HUGE SUCCESS.
MAID TO ORDER
The Story of a Domestic Worker and her Grossly Unfair Madam
...ALSO IN OUR STUDIO, IS THE SUBJECT OF HER BOOK... MADAM FROM HELL, GWEN ANDERSON.
Gwen Anderson
Madam From Hell
...ALL THIS AND MORE... TONIGHT... ON FELICIA!
MADAM FROM WHERE?!
©RAPID PHASE-1997 http://www.mg.co.za/mg/

EVE... DO YOU THINK YOU'VE BEEN TOO HARSH ON GWEN IN YOUR BOOK?
NOT AT ALL, FELICIA. SHE WAS DEFINITELY THE MADAM FROM HELL.
©RAPID PHASE-1997 http://www.mg.co.za/mg/
EXCUSE ME, BUT THE REASON I AGREED TO BE ON THIS TV SHOW WAS TO GET A FAIR HEARING... TO CLEAR MY NAME!
RIGHT. LET'S SEE WHAT OUR STUDIO AUDIENCE THINKS!
MADAM FROM HELL!
MADAM FROM HELL!
MADAM FROM HELL!
MADAM FROM HELL!
IF SHE EVER FINISHES THAT BOOK, WE'RE IN BIG TROUBLE.

I'M SORRY, MS. SISULU, BUT AFTER CAREFUL CONSIDERATION WE HAVE TO TURN YOU DOWN. WE CAN'T PUBLISH YOUR NOVEL.
WHAT? WHY?!
A "MADAM FROM HELL" WHO DOES NOTHING BUT GO SHOPPING, WATCH TV AND THEN ACCUSES THE MAID OF STEALING THE COFFEE AND SUGAR?
...AN EIGHTY YEAR OLD "MOTHER FROM ENGLAND" WHO DRINKS FIVE GIN & TONICS A DAY AND THEN CHASES MIELIE LADIES AROUND THE BLOCK?!
©RAPID PHASE-1997 http://www.mg.co.za/mg/
I'M AFRAID THESE CHARACTERS ARE JUST TOO UNBELIEVABLE.

MADAM & Eve
BY S.FRANCIS, H.DUGMORE & RICO
OUR GUEST TONIGHT IS NEWLY-APPOINTED CEO OF THE SOUTH AFRICAN POLICE SERVICE, MEYER KAHN.
MISTER KAHN...AS THE FORMER HEAD OF SOUTH AFRICAN BREWERIES, WHAT'S THE FIRST THING YOU'LL DO AS CHIEF OF POLICE?
DRAUGHT MORE COPS! I WANT MORE POLICE AVAILABLE ON TAP!
AND ANOTHER THING: THERE'LL BE NO MORE OFFICERS TRAVELLING IN PAIRS. FROM NOW ON, PATROLS WILL BE AVAILABLE IN HANDY, ECONOMIC SIX-PACKS.
UH, WHAT ABOUT THE CRIMINALS THEMSELVES, SIR?
I WANT TO PUT A CAP ON CRIME. THERE'LL BE LOTS OF MUG SHOTS!!
AND THAT'S NOT ALL! ANYONE CAUGHT FERMENTING VIOLENCE WILL BE IN BIG TROUBLE!
...DON'T YOU MEAN... "FOMENTING" VIOLENCE?
YES!...FOAM! A GOOD HEAD OF FOAM IS VERY IMPORTANT!
UH, MISTER KAHN. SOME PEOPLE MIGHT SAY THAT YOU'VE SPENT TOO LONG IN THE BEER INDUSTRY TO UNDERSTAND LAW ENFORCEMENT.
ABSOLUTELY NOT! POLICING IS LIKE ANY BUSINESS! I'LL HOP TO IT AND GULP DOWN THE CHALLENGE! I'LL SEND A CLEAR, RICH AMBER MESSAGE TO ALL CRIMINALS!
WHAT ABOUT YOUR RELATIONSHIP WITH COMMISSIONER FIVAZ? HOW IS IT?
NOT SO GOOD. RIGHT NOW WE'RE AT LAGERHEADS.
UH... DON'T YOU MEAN... "LOGGERHEADS," SIR?
DAMMIT, MAN! ALL I'M SAYING IS THAT THERE'S TROUBLE BREWING AND WE'VE GOT TO OPEN ALL THE BOTTLENECKS!

MADAM & Eve
BY S.FRANCIS, H.DUGMORE & RICO
OOOF!
BONK!
SORRY.
RACIST.
WHAT DID YOU CALL ME?
A RACIST.
BECAUSE I ACCIDENTALLY BUMP INTO YOU IN A CROWDED SHOPPING MALL?!
ADMIT IT! YOU SINGLED ME OUT BECAUSE I'M BLACK!
OKAY, THEN. SUPPOSE I RANDOMNLY BUMP INTO SOME WHITE PEOPLE? WOULD THAT HELP?
HMMM... FRANKLY, I THINK THAT WOULD GO A LONG WAY TO PROVING YOUR CREDIBILITY.
OW! YOU CRAZY OLD BAG!!
WHACK!!
AGEIST.
SEXIST.
©RAPID PHASE-1997
LISTEN. I'D LIKE TO APOLOGISE. MAYBE... I WAS WRONG TO HASTILY LABEL SOMEONE... ESPECIALLY WHEN I HARDLY KNOW THEM.
I AGREE.
EXCUSE ME. COMING THROUGH.
A BASSIST.
YOU CAN SPOT THEM A MILE AWAY.

OKAY H-HOLD IT! EVERYBODY ST...
STI-- STI-- STI-- STI-- STI--
STI-- STI-- STI-- S--STICK-- --EM--
VROOM!
©RAPID PHASE-1997
ONE GOOD THING ABOUT THIS COLD WEATHER ... IT CUTS DOWN ON HIJACKING.
...UP! S-STICK 'EM UP!!

WHEN IT COMES TO WINTER, THERE'S NOTHING LIKE A FLUFFY PILLOW, A LARGE BLANKET... AND A PORTABLE HEATER.
AHHH.
©RAPID PHASE-1997 http://www.mg.co.za/mg/
THAT'S ODD. IT'S SUDDENLY VERY CHILLY IN HERE.

CLUNK
©RAPID PHASE-1997
BONK
http://www.mg.co.za/mg/
CAN SOMEONE PLEASE TURN UP THE HEAT IN HERE ?!!

WATCH THIS, EVE.
WATCH WHAT?
IT'S THE STRANGEST THING. EVERY NIGHT WHEN IT'S FREEZING COLD THAT SQUATTER CAMP GETS ELECTRICITY.
YAY!!
I WONDER WHERE THEY GET IT FROM?
GET WHAT FROM?
©RAPID PHASE - 1997
http://www.mg.co.za/mg/

WHAT'S WRONG WITH EVE?
ALL THIS FREEZING WEATHER GAVE HER A COLD.
SNIFF
WHY IS IT THAT WHENEVER EVE HAS A COLD, IT REMINDS ME OF LABOUR UNIONS?
LABOUR UNIONS?
AH... AH... AH... AH...
COSATU!!
©RAPID PHASE - 1997
http://www.mg.co.za/mg/

SNIFF SORRY DADAM.
I GAN'T WORK DOODAY.
I GOD A DEWWIBLE CODE IN MY NODE.
WAS THAT ZULU OR XHOSA?
ENGLISH, EVE! TALK ENGLISH!
©RAPID PHASE - 1997
http://www.mg.co.za/mg/

IF YOU LEND ME FIVE RAND, I'LL EASILY BE ABLE TO PAY YOU BACK NEXT WEEK.
SURE YOU WILL.
©RAPID PHASE-1997 http://www.mg.co.za/mg/
FINE! IF YOU DON'T BELIEVE ME, READ THIS. IT CAME IN THE POST TODAY.
"CONGRATULATIONS. YOU MAY HAVE ALREADY WON A MILLION RANDS."
YOU SEE? I MAY HAVE ALREADY WON A **MILLION RANDS** AND **YOU'RE** WORRIED ABOUT A LOUSY FIVE **BUCKS**?!

YEP. ACCORDING TO THIS LETTER, I **MAY** HAVE ALREADY WON A MILLION **RANDS**.
WHICH RAISES A FEW QUESTIONS: **WHERE** DID I WIN IT, **WHEN** DID I WIN IT, AND **WHY** DIDN'T THEY COME AND NOTIFY ME RIGHT AWAY INSTEAD OF SENDING A LETTER?
EXACTLY! SO WHAT DOES THAT TELL YOU?!
©RAPID PHASE-1997 http://www.mg.co.za/mg/
...THAT WHOEVER OWES ME A MILLION BUCKS HAS A **LOT** OF EXPLAINING TO DO.

BY THE WAY. I'M A MILLIONAIRE.
MMM HMM...
IT'S TRUE! LISTEN TO WHAT CAME IN THE POST! "CONGRATULATIONS! YOU MAY HAVE ALREADY WON A **MILLION RAND!**"
"**MAY HAVE!**" THAT'S HOW THEY TRICK YOU! YOU **MAY** HAVE WON-- OR YOU MAY HAVE **NOT**!!
©RAPID PHASE-1997 http://www.mg.co.za/mg/
THAT'S OKAY. I CAN LIVE WITH A FIFTY-FIFTY CHANCE.

WHEN I COLLECT MY **MILLION RANDS**, I THINK I'LL BUY A BIG HOUSE.
GOOD.
I'LL DONATE LOTS OF MONEY TO CHARITY.
MMM HMMM.
AND DON'T WORRY. I WOULDN'T FORGET **YOU**.
THANK YOU.
©RAPID PHASE-1997 http://www.mg.co.za/mg/
HOW MUCH WOULD IT COST TO KEEP YOU IN GIN & TONICS FOR A YEAR?

HELLO. I'D LIKE TO OPEN A BANK ACCOUNT AND DEPOSIT THIS LETTER.
LETTER?
"CONGRATULATIONS. YOU **MAY** HAVE ALREADY WON A **MILLION RANDS**.
DON'T WORRY ABOUT A THING. WE **MAY** HAVE ALREADY OPENED UP A BANK ACCOUNT AND WE MAY HAVE ALREADY SENT YOU YOUR CHEQUEBOOK.
©RAPID PHASE-1997 http://www.mg.co.za/mg/
SEE? MONEY TALKS.

LOOK WHAT CAME IN THE POST!..."CONGRATULATIONS! YOU MAY HAVE ALREADY WON A MILLION RANDS!"
--THEN AGAIN, YOU MAY HAVE **NOT**.
I THINK I'LL CELEBRATE. EVE--BRING ME A GIN & TONIC!
CONGRATULATIONS! I MAY HAVE ALREADY BROUGHT YOU ONE.
©RAPID PHASE-1997 http://www.mg.co.za/mg/
THEN AGAIN, I MAY HAVE NOT.

MADAM & Eve
BY S.FRANCIS, H.DUGMORE & RICO
NO MONEY
NO MONEY
NO MONEY NO JOB
NO MONEY NO JOB
NO MONEY NO JOB NO HOME
NO MONEY NO JOB
NO MONEY NO JOB NO HOME
NO MONEY NO JOB NO HOME
NO MONEY NO JOB NO HOME and NO FRIENDS
NO FRIENDS NO FAMILY
NO FAMILY NO HOPE
NO SYMPATHY
NO MORE MISTER NICE GUY
©RAPID PHASE - 1997
NO SMOKING
NOW THERE IS SOMETHING YOU DON'T SEE EVERY DAY.

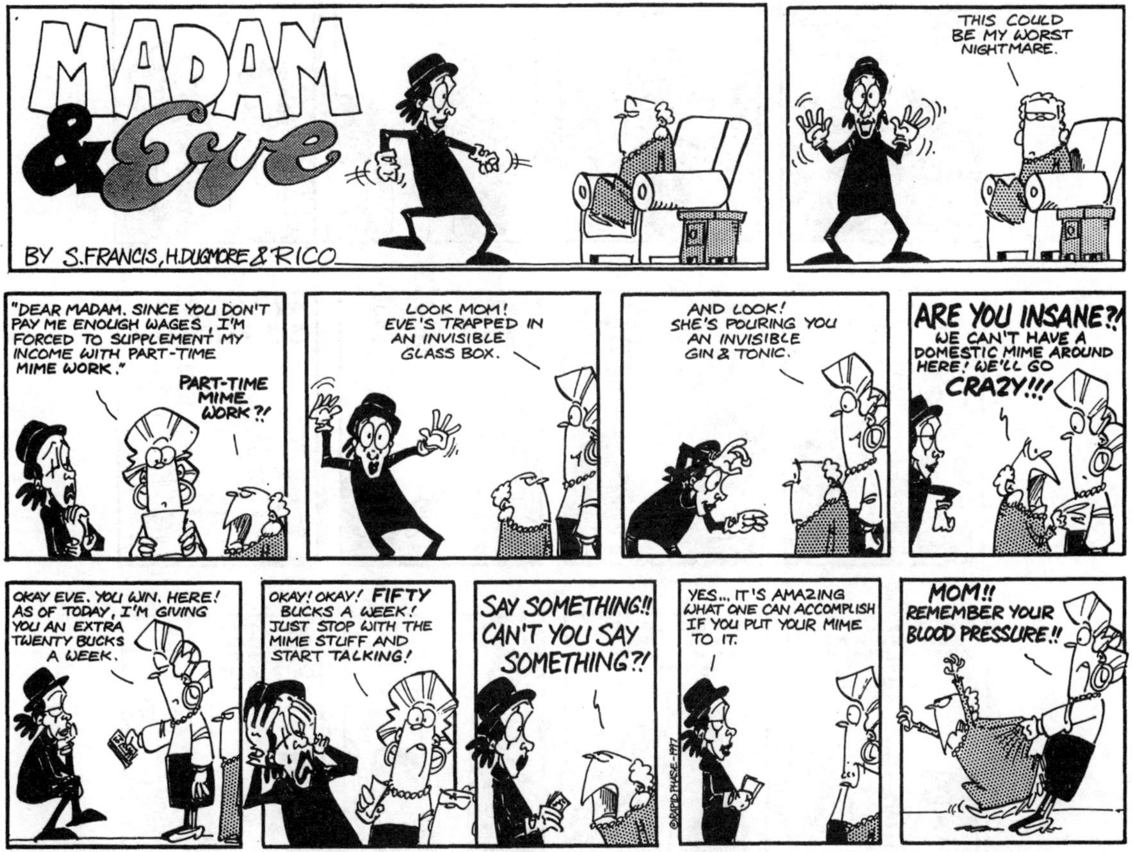
MADAM & Eve
BY S.FRANCIS, H.DUGMORE & RICO
THIS COULD BE MY WORST NIGHTMARE.
"DEAR MADAM. SINCE YOU DON'T PAY ME ENOUGH WAGES, I'M FORCED TO SUPPLEMENT MY INCOME WITH PART-TIME MIME WORK."
PART-TIME MIME WORK?!
LOOK MOM! EVE'S TRAPPED IN AN INVISIBLE GLASS BOX.
AND LOOK! SHE'S POURING YOU AN INVISIBLE GIN & TONIC.
ARE YOU INSANE?! WE CAN'T HAVE A DOMESTIC MIME AROUND HERE! WE'LL GO CRAZY!!!
OKAY EVE. YOU WIN. HERE! AS OF TODAY, I'M GIVING YOU AN EXTRA TWENTY BUCKS A WEEK.
OKAY! OKAY! FIFTY BUCKS A WEEK! JUST STOP WITH THE MIME STUFF AND START TALKING!
SAY SOMETHING!! CAN'T YOU SAY SOMETHING?!
YES... IT'S AMAZING WHAT ONE CAN ACCOMPLISH IF YOU PUT YOUR MIME TO IT.
MOM!! REMEMBER YOUR BLOOD PRESSURE!!

YOUR MOM SAYS SHE HAS A NEW HOBBY.
GOOD! WHATEVER IT IS, I'M GLAD SHE HAS SOMETHING TO KEEP HER BUSY.
I'M GOING OUT AGAIN. BE BACK SOON.
OKAY MOM. HAVE FUN.

COULD SOMEONE GIVE ME A RIDE TO THE BANK?
MOM-WHAT DO YOU THINK YOU'RE DOING?
SIMPLE. I'M PROTESTING AGAINST ALL THE CRIME IN THIS COUNTRY!
BY ROBBING A BANK?!!
HEY-IF YOU CAN'T BEAT 'EM, JOIN 'EM.
MOM! GET BACK HERE RIGHT NOW!!
EAT RUBBER DARTS, SUCKER!
PTOO!!
PTOO!!
PTOO!!

OKAY FREEZE! I'M PROTESTING AGAINST EXCESSIVE CRIME IN THIS COUNTRY! HAND OVER ALL THE MONEY IN THE BANK!
ER...THE BANK'S NEXT DOOR. THIS IS A BOTTLE STORE.
OKAY! THEN HAND OVER ALL YOUR GIN & TONIC!

NEXT! CAN I HELP YOU?
BANK
http://www.mg.co.za/mg/
YES. I'M PROTESTING AGAINST ALL THE CRIME IN THIS COUNTRY! --STICK 'EM UP!
EDITH?...IS THAT YOU?!
DAMN.
©RAPID PHASE-1997
NEVER ROB A BANK YOU LIVE TWO BLOCKS AWAY FROM.
LOOK EVERYONE! EDITH'S ROBBING OUR BANK!
HI EDITH!

THIS BANK IS PERFECT. NOBODY KNOWS ME HERE.
BAN
©RAPID PHASE-1997
EVERYONE FREEZE!! THIS IS A PROTEST AGAINST THE EXCESSIVE CRIME IN THIS COUNTRY! STICK 'EM UP AND GIVE ME ALL YOUR MONEY!!
HEY! WAIT YOUR TURN! WE WERE HERE FIRST!
http://www.mg.co.za/mg/
NO WAY! WE WERE HERE FIRST!
MOM?! IS THAT YOU?!
UH-OH.

FREEZE!! POLICE!!
WAIT A MINUTE, OFFICERS! YOU DON'T UNDER-STAND!
BANK
MY MOTHER'S NOT REALLY A BANK ROBBER! SHE'S JUST PROTESTING THE HIGH CRIME RATE AND THE COMPLETE INABILITY OF THE POLICE TO DO ANYTHING ABOUT IT!
OH! THAT EXPLAINS EVERYTHING!
©RAPID PHASE-1997 http://www.mg.co.za/mg/

IT'S NOT MY FAULT WE'RE IN JAIL! YOU'RE THE ONE WHO INSULTED THE POLICE OFFICER!
WHAT'S WRONG?
I CAN'T BELIEVE IT! I CALLED EVERYONE WE KNOW TO BAIL US OUT AND NOBODY'S HOME!!
©RAPID PHASE-1997 http://www.mg.co.za/mg/
SIGH
IT LOOKS LIKE WE HAVE NO CHOICE.
NO! DON'T TELL ME YOU'RE... YOU'RE...
RING
RING
THIS BETTER BE IMPORTANT.

ISN'T THIS EXCITING, BEING IN A REAL JAIL?
HI. WE'RE THE ANDER-SONS. WE ROB BANKS.
MOM!!
SO. WHAT ARE YOU IN FOR?
I WAS BUSTED FOR TURNING TRICKS.
©RAPID PHASE-1997 http://www.mg.co.za/mg/
SHE'S A PROFESSIONAL MAGICIAN.

GUARD! WHY AM I ALONE IN THIS CELL?! WHAT HAPPENED TO ALL THE OTHER INMATES?
APPARENTLY, THEY'VE ALL ESCAPED.
ESCAPED?! HOW DID THEY DO THAT?!
CREAK!
©RAPID PHASE-1997 http://www.mg.co.za/mg/
OH.
OKAY! WHO LEFT THE CELL DOOR OPEN AGAIN?!!

SIGH
ONE OF THOSE SPECIAL MOMENTS THAT MAKE LIFE WORTH LIVING.
SAY CHEESE.
©RAPID PHASE-1997 http://www.mg.co.za/mg/
CLICK.
AFTER SHE BAILS US OUT, I SAY WE KILL HER.

Pick'n Pay
SMASH'N GRAB

MADAM & Eve
BY S.FRANCIS, H.DUGMORE & RICO
AND NOW WE RETURN WITH MORE GREAT INTERNATIONAL TEST MATCH RUGBY...FEATURING THE SOUTH AFRICAN SPRINGBOKS --
YAY!!
...VS THE BRITISH LIONS.
YAY!!
MOM. YOU SHOULD BE ASHAMED OF YOURSELF.
YOU MIGHT BE ORIGINALLY FROM ENGLAND... BUT SOUTH AFRICA IS NOW YOUR ADOPTED HOME.
YOU'RE RIGHT.
... AND SOUTH AFRICA KICKS OFF THE MATCH!
GO BOKS!
IT'S A RUCK! ...THE LIONS HAVE GAINED POSSESSION!
GO LIONS!!
IT'S A FUMBLE! SOUTH AFRICA INTERCEPTS THE BALL!!
GO BOKS!!
...A CRUNCHING LIONS TACKLE STOPS THE ATTACK-- BUT WAIT! IT'S A PENALTY FOR THE SPRINGBOKS!
GO LIONS! GO BOKS!!
GO BOKS LIONS!! GO LION BOKS!! BOKSLIONSBOKS!
GO BLIONS!! GO LOKS!!
I'M AFRAID IT'S TEST MATCH SCHIZOPHRENIA, DOCTOR.
BETTER PUT HER ON THE COUCH.

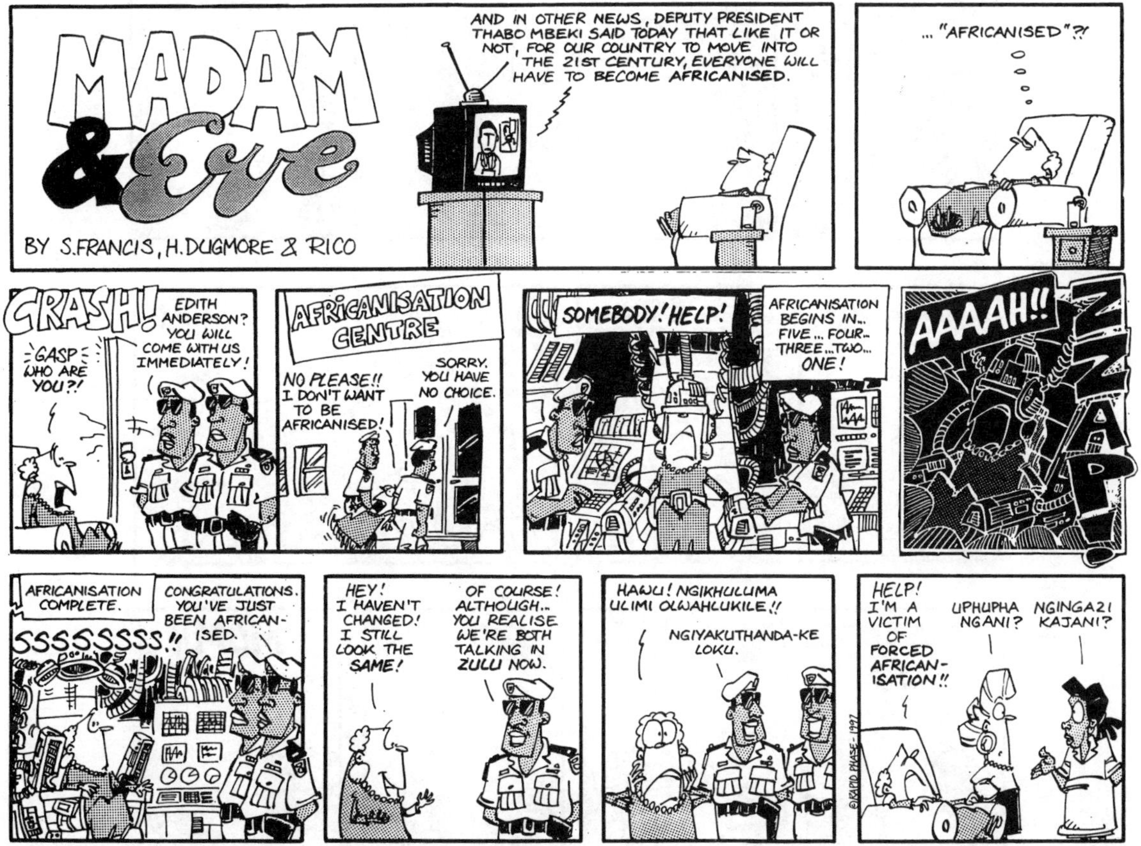
MADAM & Eve
BY S.FRANCIS, H.DUGMORE & RICO
AND IN OTHER NEWS, DEPUTY PRESIDENT THABO MBEKI SAID TODAY THAT LIKE IT OR NOT, FOR OUR COUNTRY TO MOVE INTO THE 21ST CENTURY, EVERYONE WILL HAVE TO BECOME AFRICANISED.
... "AFRICANISED"?!
CRASH!
GASP WHO ARE YOU?!
EDITH ANDERSON? YOU WILL COME WITH US IMMEDIATELY!
AFRICANISATION CENTRE
NO PLEASE!! I DON'T WANT TO BE AFRICANISED!
SORRY. YOU HAVE NO CHOICE.
SOMEBODY! HELP!
AFRICANISATION BEGINS IN.. FIVE... FOUR.. THREE...TWO... ONE!
AAAAH!!
ZZAP!
AFRICANISATION COMPLETE.
SSSSSSSS!!
CONGRATULATIONS. YOU'VE JUST BEEN AFRICAN-ISED.
HEY! I HAVEN'T CHANGED! I STILL LOOK THE SAME!
OF COURSE! ALTHOUGH.. YOU REALISE WE'RE BOTH TALKING IN ZULU NOW.
HAWU! NGIKHULUMA ULIMI OLWAHLUKILE!!
NGIYAKUTHANDA-KE LOKU.
©RAPID PHASE-1997
HELP! I'M A VICTIM OF FORCED AFRICAN-ISATION!!
UPHUPHA NGANI?
NGINGAZI KAJANI?

MADAM! A LIMO JUST PULLED UP!
I CAN'T BELIEVE IT! WE'RE THE FIRST STOP ON EVANDER HOLYFIELD'S TOUR OF SOUTH AFRICA!
DING DONG!
THAT'S HIM! AND BE CAREFUL WHAT YOU SAY!... THEY TELL ME HE'S VERY SENSITIVE ABOUT THE TYSON INCIDENT!
EVANDER!
...EDITH?
I CAN'T BELIEVE YOU EARMARKED US FOR A WHOLE AFTERNOON!
SAY WHAT?
©RAPID PHASE-1997 http://www.mg.co.za/mg/

THIS IS AMAZING! EVANDER HOLYFIELD... RIGHT HERE IN OUR OWN LOUNGE!
ER, BY THE WAY... EVANDER'S VERY SENSITIVE ABOUT HIS LAST FIGHT ...SO WHATEVER YOU DO, DON'T MENTION ANYTHING ABOUT MIKE TYSON OR YOU-KNOW-WHAT.
SO, EDITH. I'M ONLY HERE FOR A FEW HOURS. WHAT SHOULD WE DO?
I DON'T KNOW, EVANDER. I THOUGHT WE'D PLAY IT BY EAR.
MOM!!
CHOKE SOB
OOPS.
©RAPID PHASE-1997 http://www.mg.co.za/mg/

I SEE I MUST REMIND YOU AGAIN. WHEN YOU TALK TO EVANDER, PLEASE DO NOT MENTION MIKE TYSON OR HIS EAR.
GOT IT.
SO, EDITH. DID YOU SEE MY FIGHT?
DID I? WHAT AN UPSET!
... AND EVERYONE THOUGHT TYSON WAS GOING TO CHEW YOU UP AND SPIT YOU OUT!
MOM!!
SOB
OOPS. I DID IT AGAIN.
©RAPID PHASE-1997 http://www.mg.co.za/mg/

GWEN! EVE! COME QUICK! EVANDER HOLYFIELD IS GIVING ME A BOXING LESSON!
READY EDITH? OKAY! PROTECT YOURSELF! GOOD! NOW JAB! JAB! --UPPERCUT!!
OW!!
WHOMP!!
©RAPID PHASE-1997 http://www.mg.co.za/mg/
I DIDN'T HURT YOU, DID I?
;GROAN; WOULD YOU MIND STANDING ON A CHAIR?

WELL,... IT'S BEEN GREAT MEETING YOU, EVANDER.
MY PLEASURE.
AND FOR MY NEXT HEAVY-WEIGHT FIGHT... I'M SENDING ALL OF YOU FRONT ROW TICKETS!
WE'LL BE THERE! HAVE THEY SET A DATE YET?
NOT YET, BUT I'LL KEEP MY EAR TO THE GROUND.
I HEAR YOU.
©RAPID PHASE-1997 http://www.mg.co.za/mg/
OOPS.
MOM!!
HE SAID IT FIRST!

MADAM & Eve
THE LOST WORLD
JOHANNESBURG CBD
FOR SALE
TO LET
TO LET
TO LET
TO LET
FOR SALE
TO LET
XXX SHOW
CLOSING DOWN SALE
NO JOB NO GUN

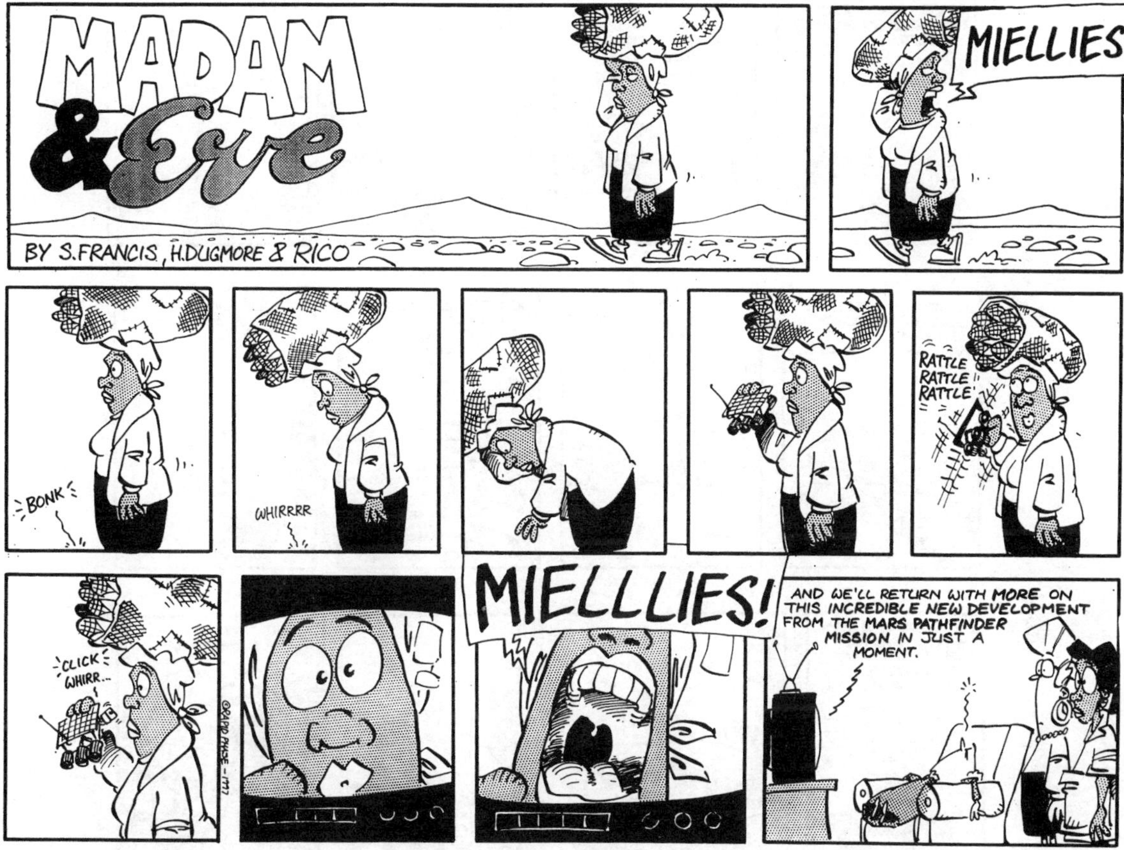
MADAM & Eve
BY S.FRANCIS, H.DUGMORE & RICO
MIELLIES!!
BONK
WHIRRRR
RATTLE RATTLE RATTLE
CLICK WHIRR...
MIELLLIES!
AND WE'LL RETURN WITH MORE ON THIS INCREDIBLE NEW DEVELOPMENT FROM THE MARS PATHFINDER MISSION IN JUST A MOMENT.

AND NOW, WE CONTINUE WITH THE FIRST LIVE TRANSMISSION FROM THE MARS PATHFINDER MISSION.
AS YOU CAN SEE, THE MARTIAN LANDSCAPE LOOKS DESERTED..., SO FAR, THERE'S ABSOLUTELY NO SIGNS OF LIFE...
WAIT A MINUTE! THERE APPEARS TO BE...YES! THERE'S SOMEONE OR SOMETHING MOVING BEHIND THAT SAND DUNE!
http://www.mg.co.za/mg/
©RAPID PHASE-1997
MIELLLIES!!

AS YOU CAN SEE, THE SOJOURNER ROBOT IS NOW EXPLORING THE MARTIAN LANDSCAPE...
WAIT A MINUTE! IT'S CHANGING DIRECTION! IT'S HEADING LEFT!
NOW IT'S HEADING RIGHT! NOW LEFT AGAIN! IT'S GOING IN CIRCLES!
©RAPID PHASE-1997
HOUSTON. WE HAVE A PROBLEM.

THE SOJOURNER ROBOT IS NOW HEADING CAREFULLY ACROSS THE MARTIAN LANDSCAPE..
http://www.mg.co.za/mg/
VROOOM!
TAXI
SCREECH!!
I ♡ ETO
BONK!
©RAPID PHASE-1997
UH, HOUSTON... DID YOU SEE THAT?
SEE WHAT?

UH, HOUSTON... WE HAVE ANOTHER PROBLEM...
AND WE'LL BE BACK...WITH MORE LIVE COVERAGE ON THE MARS PATHFINDER MISSION AFTER THIS...
EVE, WHERE'S MY GIN & TONIC?!
WHIRRRRRRR...
"SCREECH!!"
THAT'S ONE SMALL STEP FOR A MAID... ONE GIANT LEAP FOR MY FREE TIME.
HOUSTON, YOU'RE NOT GONNA BELIEVE THIS.

KNOCK KNOCK
COME IN.
EXCUSE ME, MISTER PRESIDENT. BUT OUR NEW CRIME CONSULTANT IS HERE TO SEE YOU.
©RAPID PHASE-1997 http://www.mg.co.za/mg/
RIGHT. SHOW HIM IN.
MAX! THANK YOU FOR COMING!
NO PROBLEM. MY COUNTRY NEEDS ME.

MAX-- WITH YOU ON MY CABINET, I THINK WE CAN TURN THIS CRIME PROBLEM AROUND.
THANK YOU, MISTER PRESIDENT.
©RAPID PHASE-1997 http://www.mg.co.za/mg/
EXCUSE ME, SIR. BEFORE YOU BEGIN, CAN I GET EITHER OF YOU A REFRESHMENT?
I'LL HAVE A BANANA MILKSHAKE.
MAKE IT TWO.

MAX - WE'VE SCHEDULED A PRESS CONFERENCE TO ANNOUNCE YOUR NEW POSTING AS GOVERNMENT CRIME CONSULTANT.
NOT SO FAST, MISTER PRESI-DENT. WE HAVEN'T DISCUSSED SALARY.
NO PROBLEM. HOW DOES TEN-THOUSAND BANANAS A MONTH SOUND?
I ACCEPT.
...ASSUMING, OF COURSE, THAT THE TERM "BANANAS"... IS A QUAINT COLLOQUIALISM DENOTING "RANDS."
©RAPID PHASE-1997 http://www.mg.co.za/mg/
DAMN. THIS GORILLA'S SMARTER THAN WE THOUGHT.
RIGHT. LET'S TALK BMW AND TRAVEL EXPENSES.

MAX...ON BEHALF OF ALL SOUTH AFRICANS, I'D LIKE TO THANK YOU FOR ACCEPTING OUR CRIME CONSULTANT POST.
GLAD TO HELP, MISTER PRESIDENT.
©RAPID PHASE-1997 http://www.mg.co.za/mg/
OH. THIS IS MY WIFE. SHE JUST HAD TO MEET YOU.
NELSON! NELSON MANDELA!!
SMACK!
HONEY, PLEASE. YOU'RE EMBARASSING ME.

NEXT QUESTION.
MISTER MAX!
MISTER MAX!
http://www.mg.co.za/mg/
YES?
MAX--AS THE GOVERNMENT'S NEW CRIME CONSULTANT, IS IT TRUE YOU'LL BE BRINGING BACK... "THE BITE PENALTY"?
YES. WE'VE BEEN DRAGGING OUR KNUCKLES FOR TOO LONG. I'M TALKING TOTAL GORILLA WARFARE.
VERY IMPRESSIVE.
©RAPID PHASE-1997
BUT LET'S NOT BEAT OUR CHESTS JUST YET. WE HAVE A LONG WAY TO GO.
MISTER MAX!
MISTER MAX!

MEET MAX THE GORILLA
Only 10 Rand
HOO! HOO! HOO!
MEET MAX THE GORILLA
YOU'VE GOT TO BE KIDDING.
MEET MAX THE
...HOO HOO HOO?
IT FELT RIGHT.
EET AX HE

MADAM & Eve
BY S.FRANCIS, H.DUGMORE & RICO
WEREN'T YOU SCARED WHEN YOU SAW THE WEAPON?
I DIDN'T HAVE TIME TO THINK. I JUST BIT HIM.
I CAN'T EVEN SLEEP AT NIGHT.
THAT DOES IT! I'M BUYING A GUN!
I SAY BRING BACK THE DEATH PENALTY!
CAN'T THE POLICE DO ANYTHING?
I FEEL LIKE A PRISONER IN MY OWN CAGE.
I THINK THE WHOLE THING'S LAUGHABLE!
HYENA. ME, I'M THINKING OF EMIGRATING.
THIS ZOO PROTECTED BY ARMED RESPONSE